The Ultimate Day Trader

A Comprehensive Guide to Profitable Trading

SIMON MALCOM

Table of Contents

Introduction 5

Chapter 1: Introduction to Day Trading 7

    How does day trading paintings? 8

    Benefits and risks 9

    Brief history of day trading 16

Chapter 2: Market Structure and Order Flow 32

    Understanding Market Makers 32

    How Market Makers Earn Profits 33

    Market Makers with the aid of Exchange 36

    Example of Market Maker 40

    Order types (limit, market, stop-loss) 42

    Market dynamics (supply and demand, order flow) ... 53

Chapter 3: Setting Up Your Trading Station 58

    Choosing a broker and platform 58

    What Technical Indicators Are Available on the Chart? 80

    Setting up charts and indicators 92

    Configuring trading software 96

Chapter 4: Chart Patterns 102

    Reversal patterns 102

    Continuation patterns 106

    Breakout patterns 113

Chapter 5: Technical Indicators 118

- Momentum indicators 128
- **Chapter 6: Trend Following** 134
  - Using indicators and chart patterns to confirm trends 137
  - Managing risk in trend following 142
- **Chapter 7: The Psychology of Trading** 149
  - Basics of Trading Psychology 150
  - How Bias Affects Trading 151
  - Improving Trading Psychology 153
  - Managing emotions 154
  - Developing a trading mindset 159
  - Building Emotional Discipline 160
- **Conclusion** 164

Disclaimer

The facts furnished on this book is for instructional purposes simplest. The author and publisher aren't financial advisors and are not liable for any economic choices made based on the information furnished in this eBook. All buying and selling includes hazard, and readers must seek expert recommendation earlier than making any trading choices.

© 2024 **SIMON MALCOM** All rights reserved.

Introduction

Day trading is an exciting and challenging way to make a dwelling, imparting the capability for sizable monetary rewards however also posing sizable dangers. As a day trader, you're a part of a pick organization of people who've selected to take manipulate in their monetary futures and capitalize on the possibilities provided with the aid of the markets.

However, success in day trading isn't always smooth. It requires a deep understanding of market dynamics, technical analysis, and danger control strategies. It additionally needs area, recognition, and a willingness to constantly analyze and adapt.

In this eBook, we can take you on a journey thru the arena of day buying and selling, supplying you with a complete manual to the techniques, strategies, and mindset required to achieve this discipline. From the fundamentals of technical evaluation to superior buying and selling strategies, chance management strategies, and psychological insights, we will cowl it all.

Our aim is to equip you with the expertise and abilities necessary to come to be a profitable day trader, able to navigate the markets with self-belief and precision. Whether you're a seasoned dealer or simply starting out, this book is designed that will help you take your trading to the following stage.

So, permit's get commenced on this journey collectively!

Chapter 1: Introduction to Day Trading

Day buying and selling is the hobby in which people have interaction in buying and selling stocks within a unmarried day, targeting to capitalize on short-time period rate actions for profit. Day buyers take advantage of those quick fluctuations in day buying and selling securities as they navigate through the non-stop ebb and waft of the stock market's short-term volatility.

Such buyers strive to capture brief possibilities offered via intra-day shifts, endeavoring to show over income from the market's inherent instability. In this realm, conventional time scales are discarded. Instead of days or even weeks marking progress, seconds and minutes end up pivotal devices for measuring success of their fast-paced transactions.

How does day trading paintings?

Day investors perform at the precept of capitalizing on short-term fluctuations in stock prices, executing buy and sell orders inside the equal buying and selling day. They frequently use borrowed budget to make bigger their funding potential, which escalates each capacity profits and risks related to their trades. To triumph as an afternoon dealer requires relentless statement of market trends and breaking information, rapid decision-making competencies focused on hypothesis, in conjunction with profound insights into numerous market elements which includes products, strategies, chance factors.

These traders often rent advanced procedures like margin buying and selling or alternatives usage to potentially raise returns or face hefty losses for that reason. Concentrating in the main on immediate rate modifications rather than lengthy-time period organization fitness signs lets in them to base choices the use of technical evaluation for predicting securities' rate actions. Day trading thus represents an elaborate level of investing that necessitates good sized knowledge coupled with enormous braveness.

Benefits and risks

The pros of day buying and selling:

Day trading gives many advantages, together with ability brief profits, flexibility, and the capacity to paintings from everywhere with internet access. Let's start through looking on the pros of day buying and selling:

High turnover of capital

A desirable day trader is able to making insane returns on the capital invested (if he or she is ideal). This requires an excessive turnover of capital.

How a whole lot?

Probably as a minimum as soon as every week your general fairness must be became over. For instance, if your capital is 1,000,000 USD, you'd purchase (or sell) at the least a million in line with week. The first-rate buyers possibly flip over their capital as soon as consistent with day.

Why is high turnover a requirement? Because of the regulation of massive numbers:

The regulation of huge numbers in day buying and selling

If you have a wonderful expectancy, you would want to turn over your capital as much as you can. This is pretty obvious.

Despite this simple reality, quite a few trader's cognizance on psychology and risk management. Yes, threat management is an vital a part of trading, but to begin with, you want to find a trading area that has a statistical wonderful expectancy "bare" earlier than you start considering control and any gain with the aid of knowing yourself.

However, my experience is that maximum buyers don't have a advantageous statistical side within the first area. No mental gain can ever replace that. How are you able to utilize the regulation of large numbers if you have no side?

Day buying and selling includes smaller drawdowns
Drawdowns are what make most buyers and traders give up. Seeing your capital reduce by way of 50% is

gut-wrenching, to mention the least. My enjoy is that most human beings start thinking their strategy even at drawdowns a good deal smaller at 20%. Then you begin doing behavioral mistakes.

Even when you have the pleasant techniques and edges you may probably have, they may now not make cash all the time. Traders forestall buying and selling good strategies because of drawdowns:
Day trading can reduce drawdowns. If you're accurate and exchange your edge(s) through the usage of the law of big numbers, you would possibly have extensively smaller drawdowns.

For instance, in the course of the terrific financial disaster in 2008/09, I had my nice period as an afternoon dealer. Perhaps counterintuitively, I made maximum of my cash at the long side, By day buying and selling you have got less threat of having negative information going against you (maximum news comes outdoor marketplace hours). This can be a bonus, despite the fact that you don't experience the tailwind from rising asset charges.

Day buyers can use leverage

If you have an aspect and you are confident you already know the dangers concerned, you would need to apply leverage – perhaps even plenty of it. Leverage for day buying and selling is essentially unfastened. Prop buying and selling gives you a few critical leverage if you can show you're any top.

Day trading offers mental and highbrow challenges

Day trading is tough, however that makes it extra profitable when you are a success!

In my opinion, the nice part of buying and selling is sipping espresso whilst trying out new thoughts. The execution of trades isn't mainly exciting, and besides, it's all automatic.

The cons of day trading

However, it additionally has some dangers, together with high volatility, mental pressure, and the need to monitor the market closely. It is essential to weigh the positives and negatives earlier than embarking on an afternoon-buying and selling adventure. If you're trading cryptocurrencies, you want to be privy to the MATIC fee that's the transaction fees of the platform you're the usage of.

Unfortunately, there are many cons and disadvantages concerned in day buying and selling. Here are some of them:

Day buying and selling doesn't take benefit of the lengthy-time period upward float:

I actually have documented the overnight facet in the stock marketplace (and the gold fee). By day buying and selling, you are not taking gain of this "low striking fruit" that exists in lots of asset training.

The chart below suggests the return by way of being invested handiest from the near the next day's open inside the S&P 500:

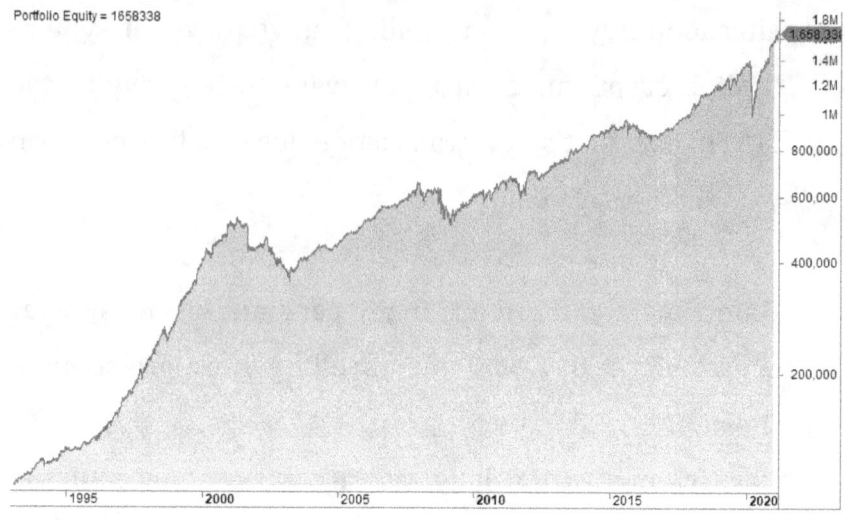

The aspect is huge.

Opposite, the common gain from the open to the near is terrible over the past 30 years. Day buying and selling is largely a zero-sum recreation.

Day trading calls for time and commitment

If you're extreme about day buying and selling, you have to commit time and capital. This has an possibility cost:

Perhaps you will be higher off just shopping for a few index price range and focusing in your day-to-day profession in a normal task?

Most day investors would sincerely be better off in the event that they focused on their everyday task.

Also, too many human beings are trying to day change while having a job. I say overlook it.

You cannot day alternate and paintings at the equal time. There is only a small chance with a view to paintings, and also you end up having an angry boss. You want to deal with it as a profession and feature a solid plan. Having a very mechanized technique might work, however you still want to allocate time within the nighttime to do studies.

Commissions and gearing can be ruinous
Gearing can be an advantage, but losses multiply in case you get it incorrect. Commissions also are ruinous in the long run.

Many believe zero fee would possibly assist the day dealer, however we will argue otherwise. The most likely end result is that you overtrade because it charges "nothing" to buy and promote.

Market noise is a large con in day trading

Most of the motion intraday is simply undeniable noise. Most of the headline information is published earlier than the opening bell, and maximum of the trading day is simply noise. The motives why investors and traders purchase and promote are countless, and it requires a wonderful intellect to discover any actual styles that can stand the take a look at of time.

You need software program resources

You also need to pay for software and buying and selling tools/information. It all provides up ultimately.

Brief history of day trading

In modern-day times, we take day buying and selling for granted. It makes feel to us that a person can buy a stock and promote it at the identical day.

However, day buying and selling is a exceptionally new idea. The records of day buying and selling has long past thru many twists and turns over time, but it has never been greater distinguished than it's far today.

When did day trading begin? How lengthy has day trading existed? Today, we're going to inform you the whole thing you need to recognize about the history of day buying and selling.

1867: Day Trading Starts with the Ticker Tape

Day buying and selling may be traced all of the manner again to 1867. Contrary to what many humans agree with, day buying and selling did no longer emerge with the rise of computers or the internet. In reality, it strains its records lower back to even before electricity.

Day trading can be traced returned to 1867. Soon after the telegraph was invented, inventory markets used the telegraph's verbal exchange generation to create the primary ticker tape. Ticker tape made it easy to talk information approximately transactions going on at the trade floor with brokers.

Before the internet and other global communique systems have been invented, agents would try to stay in near proximity to exchanges just like the New York Stock Exchange, as it supposed they have been getting a consistent deliver of ticker tape with the maximum updated records.

Today, ticker tape refers back to the stream of digital information streaming throughout a banner. In days long gone by way of, it became a physical sheet of paper. Brokers could use ticker tape to make knowledgeable selections on stock market movements at some point of the day, taking into account some agents to take part in day buying and selling.

Throughout the early records of inventory markets, person buyers did now not have direct get admission to markets. All orders had been placed thru a dealer. Brokers used statistics accumulated off the ticker tape.

This shape of trading became commonplace for the duration of the early days of stock markets. However, the limitations to access meant day trading was now not famous among the overall population.

1971: A Communication Network is Created
In 1971, the spread of stock market data round the arena became extra green than ever before. That 12

months, the National Association of Securities Dealers (NASD) created an electronic communique network (ECN). That ECN become known as the National Association of Securities Dealers Automated Quotation System. Today, we understand it as the NASDAQ.

An ECN is defined as any laptop machine that helps financial merchandise trades outside of inventory exchanges. This helped to open stock markets and making an investment to individual buyers – no longer just brokers.

Suddenly, all styles of buying and selling – along with day buying and selling – had been extra on hand to the common guy. However, it was nonetheless a protracted approach away from becoming a famous or commonplace hobby among smalltime, individual traders.

1975: Fixed Commission Exchanges Are Abolished
For the complete early history of American stock markets (180 years), there had been constant quotes on trades. Markets had fixed costs on all trades, which

meant that agents couldn't compete with other brokers on fee.

In 1975, that changed – and changed the stock marketplace world all the time. That year, the Securities and Exchange Commission (SEC) installed regulations abolishing fixed commissions.

That meant, for the first time in one hundred eighty years, buying and selling prices on inventory markets were determined by means of market opposition – which looks like the ideal manner to decide matters associated with the stock market.

In reaction to these adjustments, Charles Schwab and different companies commenced permitting customers to trade shares at discounted fee fees, marking the start of the cut price dealer generation. Brokers started out to compete with one another by way of providing lower and decrease charges. These agents began to innovate and experiment with new buying and selling structures that made the process greater green.

ECNs Make Trading Easier for the Average Investor

A number of Electronic Communication Networks (ECNs) might seem over the approaching years, inclusive of famous names like Instinet (which still exists to this day, and become virtually founded earlier than NASDAQ, in 1969).

These ECNs arose to address the call for of traders. Driven by using a brand new technology of aggressive commission prices, ECNs had been able to serve a growing range of clients. ECNs had a primary role in the marketplace: they were automated structures that matched buy and promote orders for securities.

More importantly, ECNs related person traders with main brokerages, allowing either aspect to shop for/sell securities from the alternative without going via a middleman. This drove expenses down even in addition, making day trading even simpler.

During this era, ECNs like Instinet, Select Net, and NYSE Arca would all end up prominent in the enterprise.

Instinet is the first-class-recognized, and was extensively used in the course of the 1970s, 80s, and 90s for NASDAQ trades. Part of its reputation became that people and small firms can also use it.

Select Net, alternatively, become used usually through market makers. To this present day, it does now not require immediate order execution. It's used to help investors exchange with unique marketplace makers.

NYSE Arca turned into an ECN that emerged out of a aggregate of the NYSE and Archipelago, an early ECN from 1996. It enables electronic inventory buying and selling on foremost US exchanges – like the NYSE and NASDAQ.

The Stock Market Crash of 1987 Makes it Even Easier to Trade

In October 1987, the inventory marketplace crashed, revealing a fundamental hassle with the manner markets worked for character traders.

What was that hassle? Well, on this time period, most trades were conducted over the phone. When the stock market crashed, brokers had an easy manner of fending off the hassle: they just stopped answering their phones. Investors might call to desperately try to promote their stocks, best to be omitted.

The SEC saw this flaw and added an alternative machine known as Small Order Entry System (SOES). This device gave orders of one,000 shares or less a priority over larger orders.

This trade helped protect character, small-time traders at the markets. Like all of the other modifications stated above, it eliminated one extra barrier to access between character traders and the stock marketplace, supporting to facilitate day buying and selling even in addition.

The Dot Come Craze of 1997 Showcases Another Problem with Markets
When you allow tens of millions of man or woman investors to easily make investments inside the stock marketplace, it famous every other fundamental market trouble: it introduces mass psychology to the stock marketplace at a stage by no means previously visible.

This become best-visible in 1997, when the dot-com craze fueled hypothesis in era stocks. The internet was just spreading to households across the developed international, and people were shopping for any stocks associated with the net.

During this term, online brokers like E-Trade released services that made it even less complicated for traders to make investments. E-Trade became particularly well-known for permitting man or woman traders to without problems take part in IPOs.

Thanks to the net, small traders now had direct get admission to to price quotes, trading activities, and other treasured market records. This leveled the gambling area for everyone. Some huge brokers even argued that the market desired small buyers, due to the fact these small traders may want to take benefit of SOES (the machine that gave small investors precedence over large buyers).

The global of tech stocks was booming, and day buying and selling changed into fast turning into a "thing" people did. It wasn't uncommon for an average investor with little marketplace revel in to make a whole lot of money on the stock marketplace by means of shopping for one inventory in the morning and then selling it inside the afternoon at 400% margin rates. Between 1997 and 2000, the NASDAQ exploded with increase, growing from 1200 to 5000.

Day Trading Continues to Expand in 1999
By 1999, day buying and selling had emerge as a full-blown phenomenon.

However, in evaluation to day trading these days, there weren't as many day investors as you're probably wondering. It changed into one of those matters that numerous human beings heard human beings did – however few "common" human beings sincerely participated in.

As testament to that reality, Arthur Levitt, Chairman of the SEC, testified earlier than Congress in 1999 and anticipated that the variety of day buyers was round 7,000.

In contrast, Mr. Levitt envisioned that there have been about 5 million internet customers subscribed to on-line agents.

Like many stuff human beings didn't apprehend, day trading have become feared and distrusted. During this time period, day trading had a terrible connotation. The bad mind-set toward day trading culminated in a capturing spree at an Atlanta day buying and selling office, in which Mark Barton killed 12 people and injured 13 extra after dropping an expected $105,000 in day buying and selling over a two-month length.

The Barton incident convinced many humans that day buying and selling turned into so traumatic it could convince an in any other case everyday guy to commit mass homicide.

Day trading as a career took any other hit when, weeks after the Barton shootings, the North American Securities Administrators Association launched a record mentioning that 7 out of 10 day investors lose the entirety. They don't simply lose money ordinary – they lose the whole thing they've invested.

2000: The SOES Advantage is Eliminated

Prior to 2000, one among the most important benefits day buyers had become SOES, the gadget that ensured that trades beneath 1,000 have been addressed earlier than trades over 1,000, giving an advantage to smaller traders. The system changed into designed to inspire individual traders to enter the marketplace, but it finally led to day buyers having an unfair gain.

In the yr. 2000, the SOES was modified. The biggest exchange changed into that it eliminated the blessings for day investors.

The Dot Com Bubble Bursts

The converting of the SOES became one discouraging turn of events for day traders. However, soon after the SOES was modified, another devastating trade happened: the dot com bubble burst.

As a result, many day traders went bankrupt or lost a big amount of their investments. Many have been scared away from the profession and sought new careers. The heyday of being a day trader seemed to be over.

This marked the cease of a completely unique era of day buying and selling. Prior to the dot com bubble's burst, day buying and selling turned into viewed like the Wild West. Day investors have been trying to make a short buck. Investors had been centered on pump and dump schemes. Regulations had been confined.

After the dot com bubble burst, however, day trading would turn out to be a great deal greater similar to everyday investing – it become something normal investors should without difficulty take part in.

Day Trading within the 2000s
The dot com bubble's burst marked the end of one length of day trading, but it become the begin of a new era of day buying and selling. Instead of "get wealthy brief" schemes and lawless frontier-fashion trading, day buying and selling within the 2000s began to have a greater professional mind-set.

HowStuffWorks.Com cites the USA Department of Labor while it says that there have been 320,000 securities, commodities, and economic provider dealers in 2006 throughout the USA, and that wide variety includes day investors. Nevertheless, we don't have a specific breakdown about the range of day traders.

As a wager, HowStuffWorks.Com estimates that 5% to ten% of expert financial carrier dealers are day investors, which might imply 16,000 to 32,000 people said their day buying and selling profits to the United States Department of Labor in 2006. However, the total number of day traders is lots higher, as newbie and element-time day buyers "may additionally number inside the thousands and thousands" (Source).

The Forex Market Trading within the 2000s
Trading overseas currencies is sort of as antique as civilization itself. However, current foreign exchange trading is a great deal more current, and simplest seemed after the cease of the Bretton Woods device within the Seventies. The end of the Bretton Woods gadget meant that the US greenback became now not pegged to the rate of gold. The technology of fixed

exchange fees become over, and it turned into a new generation of fluctuating trade rates.

Why am I telling you this in an editorial about the records of day trading?

Well, foreign exchange and day trading move hand in hand. As foreign exchange (forex) trading became more not unusual, so too did day buying and selling.

TradingAcademy.Com reports that during 1980, forex trades brought up to $70 billion a day in overall value. By 2003, that range had accelerated to $2. Four trillion an afternoon.

Most foreign exchange buyers do not participate in day trading. Currency markets not often vary widely enough to make a great profit through day buying and selling. However, many investors take part in brief-term foreign exchange trades, or use forex as one part of their day trading enterprise.

Where Does Day Trading Go from Here?

Today, day trading stays a famous pastime amongst each professional buyers and amateurs. Some human beings will tell you day buying and selling is a volatile interest, while others will convince you that it's an smooth manner to get wealthy short. The fact is someplace in among, and it largely relies upon to your skill as an person investor.

Your ability as a day dealer is closely linked in your ability as a universal investor. It requires notable research and analytical abilities – and a honest bit of good fortune. Modern markets aren't best uneven, but they also circulate fast. Whether you're looking at a ten-minute period or a ten-month period, trading over the previous couple of years has been a rocky avenue.

Today's day traders use current research tools and algorithms in an effort to time the market. Forms of day buying and selling – like binary alternatives trading and foreign exchange trading – have end up synonymous with "rip-off" within the on-line global, as determined people search for any manner to make a quick greenback at the internet.

Chapter 2: Market Structure and Order Flow

The term market maker refers to a company or character who actively rates two-sided markets in a specific security through supplying bids and gives (known as asks) alongside the marketplace size of each. Market makers offer liquidity and intensity to markets and take advantage of the distinction within the bid-ask spread. They can also make trades for his or her personal money owed, which can be called predominant trades.

Understanding Market Makers

Many marketplace makers are regularly brokerage houses that offer buying and selling offerings for buyers with the intention to preserve financial markets liquid. A market maker also can be an man or woman dealer, who's generally called a nearby. The massive majority of market makers paintings on behalf of massive institutions because of the scale of securities needed to facilitate the extent of purchases and income.

Each marketplace maker presentations purchase and promote quotations for a guaranteed number of stocks. Once the marketplace maker receives an order from a buyer, they at once sell off their function of shares from their personal inventory. This lets in them to finish the order.

A marketplace maker must decide to constantly quoting prices at which it's going to buy (or bid for) and promote (or ask for) securities.1

Market makers have to also quote the extent in which they're inclined to change along with the frequency of time they will quote on the pleasant bid and excellent provide prices. Market makers have to stick to those parameters always and all through all market outlooks. When markets become erratic or risky, market makers have to continue to be disciplined with a view to retain facilitating smooth transactions.

How Market Makers Earn Profits

Market makers are compensated for the risk of preserving belongings because they will see a decline inside the price of a safety after it has been purchased from a vendor and earlier than it is offered to a purchaser.

Consequently, they typically charge the aforementioned unfold on every safety they cowl. For example, while an investor searches for a stock the usage of an online brokerage company, it would examine a bid fee of $one hundred and an ask price of $one hundred.05. This method the broker purchases the inventory for $a hundred, then sells it to prospective customers for $100.05. Through high-quantity buying and selling, a small unfold can upload as much as massive day by day income.

Market makers have to perform under a given alternate's bylaws, which are accepted by a country's securities regulator, such as the Securities and Exchange Commission (SEC).2

The rights and responsibilities of marketplace makers range by way of change and by using the form of monetary tool they change, consisting of equities or options.

Market Makers vs. Designated Market Makers (DMMs)

Many exchanges use a machine of marketplace makers, who compete to set the fine bid or provide so as to win the commercial enterprise of incoming orders. But some entities, such as the New York Stock Exchange (NYSE), have what's referred to as a designated market maker (DMM) gadget alternatively.

Once referred to as specialist systems, DMMs are basically lone market makers with a monopoly over the order float in a specific safety or securities. Because the NYSE is a public sale market, bids and asks are competitively forwarded through investors.3

Here's how it works: The expert posts these bids and asks for the whole market to see and ensures they may be said in an accurate and well timed manner. They additionally ensure that the pleasant charge is constantly maintained, that all marketable trades are executed, and that order is maintained on the floor.

The expert has to also set the opening fee for the stock every morning, that can vary from the day gone bee's remaining price primarily based on after-hours information and activities. The professional determines the proper market charge primarily based on deliver and call for

Market Makers with the aid of Exchange

As referred to above, market makers offer trading offerings for investors who take part in the securities marketplace. Their sports via their entity trading debts produce and enhance liquidity inside the markets. You can discover those entities all over the worldwide market. We've highlighted a number of the most famous ones in exclusive elements of the world.

NYSE and Nasdaq

The NYSE and Nasdaq are the 2 primary inventory exchanges inside the United States. Both are primarily based in New York.

According to the NYSE, a lead market maker is an "ETP holder or firm that has registered" to trade securities with the alternate.6

Over on the Nasdaq, a marketplace maker is a "member organization that buys and sells securities at fees it presentations in NASDAQ for its very own account (foremost trades) and for purchaser bills (organization trades)."7

Some of the top names of market makers in New York encompass:

Credit Suisse
Deutsche Bank
Goldman Sachs
KCG Americas
Timber Hill 6

Frankfurt Stock Exchange (FRA)

The Frankfurt Stock Exchange (FRA) is one in every of seven stock exchanges in Germany. It is also the biggest inside the united states. The alternate, that is operated by means of Deutsche Börse AG, calls its marketplace makers distinct sponsors. Eight

The following are a number of the names of market makers on Extra, that is the digital buying and selling platform of the alternate group:

Berenberg

JPMorgan

Morgan Stanley

Optiver

UBS Europe9

London Stock Exchange Group

London is domestic to one in every of the most important inventory trade groups in Europe. The London Stock Exchange (LSE) is part of the London Stock Exchange Group. This institution also consists of the own family of FTSE Russell Indexes and the group's clearing services.10

The following are some of the important thing marketplace makers in this part of the arena:

BNP Paribas

GMP Securities Europe

Liberium Capital

Mediobanca

Standard Charteredeleven

Tokyo Exchange Group

The Tokyo Exchange Group mixed the Tokyo Stock Exchange and the Osaka Securities Exchange into one unit in 2013. In addition to infrastructure and information, the organization presents "market customers with reliable venues for buying and selling listed securities and derivatives units."12

According to JPX, the following are some of the key names among marketplace makers:

ABN AMRO Clearing
Nissan Securities
Nomura Securities
Phillip Securities
Societe Generale13
Toronto Stock Exchange (TSX)
Toronto is taken into consideration to be Canada's monetary capital, that's where the united states of America's main inventory alternate is located. The Toronto Stock Exchange (TSX), that's the united states' biggest alternate, is owned via TMX Group.

The TSX lists the following among its market makers:
BMO Nesbitt Burns

Integral Wealth Solutions

Questrade

Scotia Capital

TD Securities14

Market-making enables a smoother glide of economic markets with the aid of making it less complicated for traders and traders to buy and promote. Without market making, there may be inadequate transactions and less investment sports.

Example of Market Maker

Here's a hypothetical example to expose how a market maker trades. Let's say there may be a marketplace maker in XYZ stock. They can also provide a quote of $10.00 - $10.05 or 100x500. This means that they make a bid (they'll buy) of $10.00 for a hundred stocks. They'll additionally offer (they will promote) 500 shares at $10.05. Other market participants may additionally then buy (lift the offer) from the MM at $10.05 or sell to them (hit the bid) at $10.00.

Who Are Market Makers and What Do They Do?

A marketplace maker participates within the securities market by means of imparting trading offerings for investors and boosting liquidity in the market. They mainly offer bids and gives for a specific protection in addition to its marketplace length. Market makers normally paintings for massive brokerage houses that profit off of the distinction among the bid and ask unfold.

How Do Market Makers Work?

A number of marketplace makers perform and compete with each different inside securities exchanges to draw the commercial enterprise of buyers with the aid of putting the most aggressive bid and ask offers. In some instances, exchanges like the NYSE use a specialist machine wherein a expert is the sole market maker who makes all the bids and asks which can be visible to the market. A specialist process is carried out to make sure that each one marketable trades are completed at a truthful rate in a well-timed manner.

How Do Market Makers Earn a Profit?

Market makers earn a profit via the spread between the securities bid and offer charge. Because market makers bear the hazard of protecting a given safety, which may drop in rate, they're compensated for this chance of maintaining the assets. For instance, don't forget an investor who sees that Apple inventory has a bid price of $50 and an ask charge of $50.10. What this means is that the marketplace maker sold the Apple shares for $50 and is selling them for $50.10, earning a profit of $0.10.

Order types (limit, market, stop-loss)

Market orders, limit orders, and prevent orders are common order types used to shop for or sell stocks and ETFs. Learn how and whilst a trader might use them.

Different order kinds can bring about hugely distinctive effects, so it's critical to understand the distinctions amongst them. Here we awareness on three fundamental order kinds—marketplace orders, restrict orders, and stop orders—and speak how they fluctuate and while to don't forget every.

It enables to suppose of every order type as a distinct device appropriate to its very own motive. Whether you're buying or promoting, it is critical to pick out your primary purpose— whether it's having your order stuffed quick at the triumphing marketplace fee or controlling the charge of your change. Then you could determine which order type is maximum suitable to attain your aim.

What is a marketplace order and how do I use it?

A market order is an order to shop for or promote an inventory on the marketplace's best to be had charge. It normally ensures an execution however does not guarantee a particular rate. When the number one intention is to execute the change right now, a marketplace order is premier. It's typically appropriate whilst you assume a stock is priced proper, while you're sure you want a fill on your order, or when you want a direct execution.

A few caveats: A stock's quote usually consists of the highest bid capacity consumers are willing to pay to collect the inventory, the lowest offer capacity sellers are willing to simply accept to promote the stock, and the remaining price at which the inventory traded. However, the remaining change fee may not necessarily be modern, particularly in the case of much less-liquid shares, whose final change may additionally have happened minutes or hours ago. This may be the case in fast-moving markets when stock costs can change significantly in a short time frame. Therefore, while setting a market order, the cutting-edge bid and offer prices are typically of more significance than the last change rate.

Market orders are normally placed while the market is already open. A marketplace order located whilst markets are closed would be finished at the following market open, which may be notably better or decrease from its previous close. Between marketplace sessions, numerous factors can impact a stock's price, which includes the discharge of profits, organization news or financial information, or surprising events that have an effect on a whole industry, region, or the marketplace as a whole.

What is a limit order and how does it paintings?
A restriction order is an order to buy or promote an inventory with a restriction at the maximum fee to be paid (with a buy limit) or the minimal rate to be received (with a promote limit). If the order is filled, it's going to most effective be at the required restrict price or better. However, there's no guarantee of execution. A

restriction order can be appropriate whilst you assume you could buy at a rate decrease than—or promote at a charge better than—the modern quote. The thinkorswim® chart under illustrates the use of market orders versus limit orders.

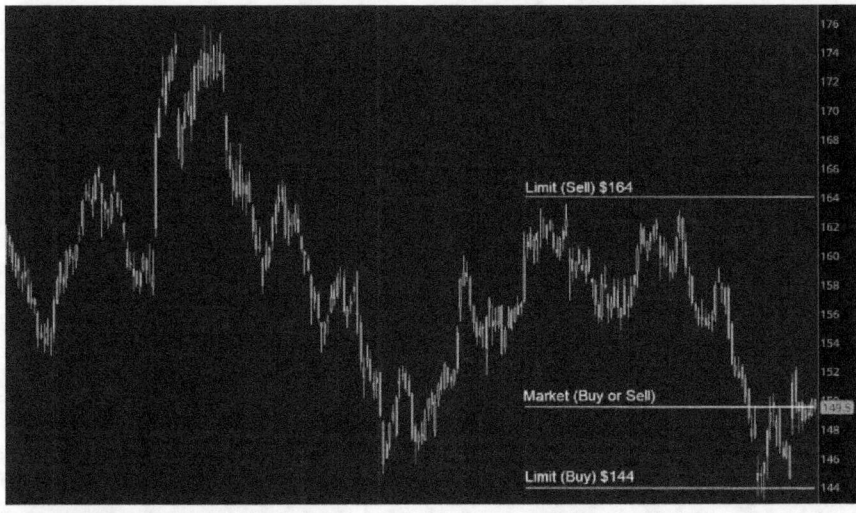

In this example, the final change fee changed into $149.50. Let's overview the scenarios for every order type:

A trader who wanted to purchase (or promote) the inventory as speedy as viable could location a marketplace order, which would in maximum cases be completed right away at or near the inventory's cutting-edge fee (white line)—supplied the marketplace turned into open while the order changed into placed and barring uncommon marketplace conditions.

A trader who desired to shop for the stock best if it dropped to $a hundred and forty-four ought to area a buy restrict order with a limit rate of $a hundred and forty-four (inexperienced line). If the stock fell to that level or decrease, the restriction order would cause and the order could be accomplished at $one hundred forty-four or less. If the stock didn't fall to $144 or much less, no execution might occur.

A trader who desired to sell the inventory if it reached $164 should place a promote restrict order with a limit fee of $164 (pink line). If the inventory rose to that level or better, the restriction order would trigger and the order might be performed at $164 or greater. If the stock didn't rise to $164 or more, no execution could occur.

Note, even though the inventory reached the desired restrict rate, the order won't fill due to the fact there may be orders in advance of yours. In that case, there might not be sufficient (or additional) dealers (or consumers) willing to sell (or buy) at that restriction price, so your order wouldn't fill. (Limit orders are usually executed on a first-come, first-served basis.) That said, it is also possible your order should fill at a good better rate. For example, a buy order ought to execute beneath a restriction rate, and a sell order could execute for more than a restrict price.

What is a forestall order, and the way is it used?
A forestall order is an order to buy or sell an inventory at the marketplace rate once the stock has traded at or through a certain rate (the "prevent rate"). If the stock reaches the forestall price, the order will become a stay marketplace order and is generally filled at the following to be had market rate. If the inventory fails to attain the stop fee, the order isn't always executed.

A prevent order may be suitable in diverse scenarios:

When a stock you already very own has risen and also you want to try and shield part of your unrealized benefit have to it start to fall.

When you latterly offered a inventory and need to set a floor around the stage of loss you'll be willing to tolerate on the position.

When you want to buy a stock need to it damage above a certain stage due to the fact you suspect that would sign the start of a persevered upward thrust.

A promote forestall order is occasionally referred to as a "stop-loss" order due to the fact it is able to be used to assist guard an unrealized benefit or searching for to decrease a loss. A promote stop order is entered at a forestall price beneath the modern-day marketplace rate. If the stock drops to the forestall charge (or trades under it), the stop order to sell is caused and turns into a market order to be done at the marketplace's current charge. A promote prevent order is not assured to execute near your stop price. A prevent order can also be used to shop for. A purchase forestall order is entered at a prevent charge above the modern market charge (in essence, "stopping" the stock from getting far from you as it rises).

Let's revisit our previous example but look at the potential effects of the usage of a prevent order to buy and a stop order to promote—with the prevent charges similar to the limit fees previously used.

While the two graphs may also look similar, note that the placement of the red and green traces is reversed: The prevent order to promote would cause whilst the inventory fee hit $144 (or less) and might be completed as a market order on the present day price. So, if the stock has been to fall similarly after hitting the forestall price, it is viable that the order might be carried out at a fee that is lower than the present rate. Conversely, for the prevent order to shop for, if the stock rate of $164 is reached, the buy prevent order may be done at a better charge.

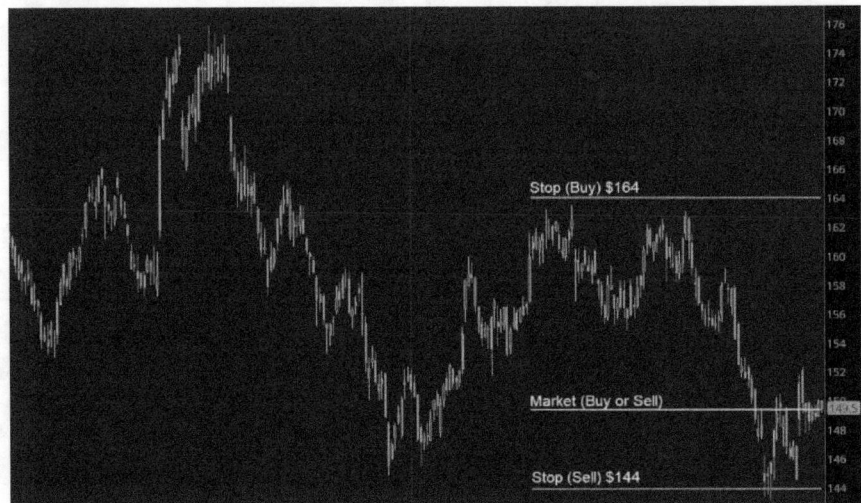

What are charge gaps?

A rate hole occurs when a stock's charge makes a sharp flow up or down without a trading going on in among. It can manifest due to elements like income announcements, a exchange in an analyst's outlook, or a information release. Gaps regularly arise when exchanges open or while information or events outdoor of buying and selling hours have created an imbalance in supply and call for.

Stop orders and charge gaps

Remember that the key distinction between a restrict order and a prevent order is that the limit order will handiest be crammed at the specified restrict charge or better; whereas, once a stop order triggers at the required price, it will likely be stuffed at the prevailing fee within the market—which means that it could be finished at a price significantly different than the prevent charge.

What is a prevent limit order?

Another order kind combines a prevent order and a limit order. The prevent restrict order specifies the fee that the order must be brought on and the price that the trader wants to execute the change. It offers the dealer a traditional stop order, however as soon as triggered, a restriction order at their distinct fee instead of a marketplace order. While the trader may opt to sell at them restrict fee, execution isn't guaranteed, and the trader has danger of the stock transferring lower after triggering.

The chart underneath indicates a inventory that "gapped down" from extra than $34 to round $32 between a previous remaining fee and the next starting fee. A forestall order to promote at a prevent fee of $34—which could trigger on the marketplace's open due to the fact the stock's fee fell beneath the stop rate and, as a marketplace order, executes at $32—can be substantially decrease than meant, and worse for the vendor. In the case of a prevent restrict order with the stop set at $34 and the restrict at $33, for example, the trader could be looking the stock exchange lower and "hoping" or "ready" for the inventory to return to $33 earlier than being accomplished.

Stop order: Gaps down can result in an unexpected lower price.

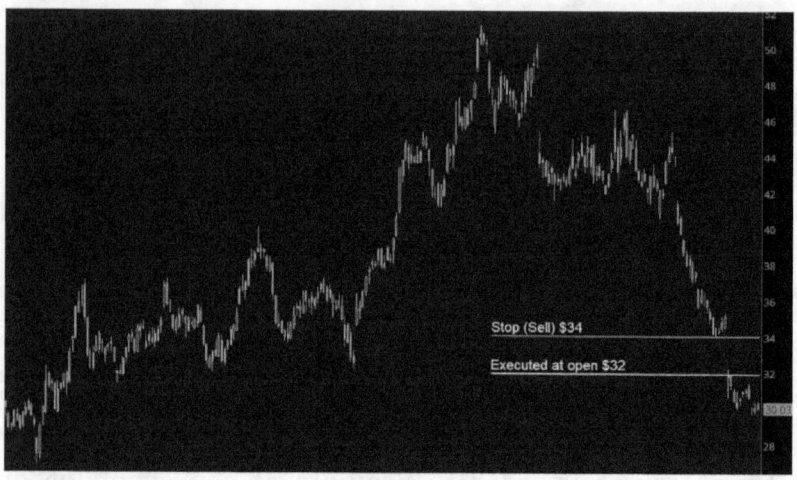

Limit orders and fee gaps

In a similar way that a "hole down" can work against you with a prevent order to sell, a "gap up" can work on your favor inside the case of a restrict order to sell. In the subsequent example, a restriction order to promote is positioned at a restrict rate of $105. The stock's prior last price turned into $104. If the inventory opened at $a hundred and ten because of tremendous information launched after the previous market's close, the exchange could be finished on the market's open at that charge—higher than predicted and higher for the vendor.

Limit order: Gap up can result in an unexpected higher price.

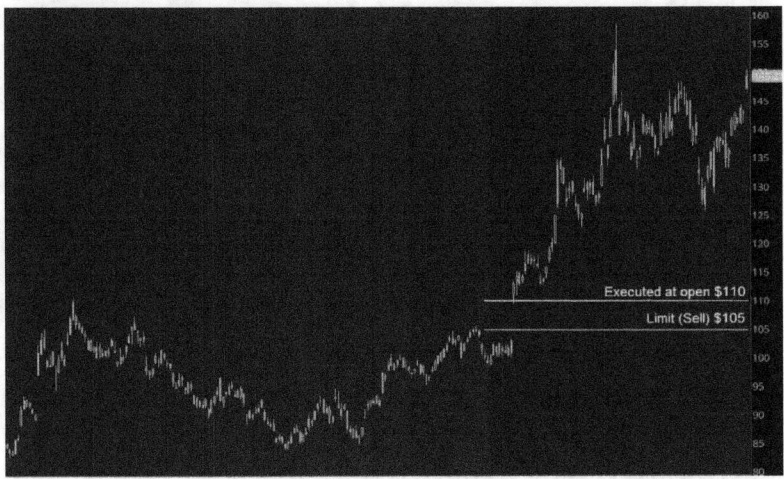

Market dynamics (supply and demand, order flow)

Understanding marketplace dynamics through deliver and demand order float evaluation is a crucial ability for investors hoping to make nicely-knowledgeable selections. Let's have a look at the concepts of supply and call for in addition to how order float evaluation can offer insights into how the marketplace features.

Essentials of Demand and Supply:

Supply:
Supply is the quantity of a economic tool that sellers are equipped to provide at numerous expenses. On a charge chart, deliver is generally represented through a vertical line that rises to higher fee factors.

2. Demand:
Demand is a degree of the amount of products that buyers are willing to purchase at special charge factors. Similar to supply, call for is proven on a price chart as a vertical line that goes from better to decrease fee tiers.

3. Peace:
When shopping for and selling interest is in balance, a rate called the equilibrium is determined through the intersection of supply and demand. Modifications to this equilibrium result in fee changes.

Order Flow Analysis:

Examination of Order Flow:

Understanding the Order Process Examining real market transactions in actual-time is important for order drift analysis. Traders examine the glide of buy and sell orders to look what factors affect price movements.

2. Market Depth:

The gift stages of deliver and call for at distinctive price factors are displayed in the order e-book, once in a while referred to as marketplace intensity. Analyzing this records makes it clean to perceive extensive ranges in which there is lots of interest in shopping for or promoting.

3. Validation of Price Action:

Price movement is a standard technique to verifying deliver and call for zones. An increase in shopping for volume at a supply region or a decrease in promoting quantity at a call for region, as an instance, may confirm the robustness of those ranges.

Practical Methods:

Establishing Critical Points:

Order glide evaluation can be used to perceive vital levels of guide and resistance where deliver and call for mismatches are possibly to occur. These stages therefore become crucial choice-making instances that decide whether or not a transaction will be successful or fail.

2. Using Confirmation Through Candlestick Patterns:

Combining order float analysis with candlestick patterns improves precision. A bullish engulfing sample close to a demand area, for instance, might be a hallmark of a capability upward growth.

3. Examination of Volume:

Volume analysis is used to confirm the dynamics of order drift. An exquisite boom in volume following the emergence of a deliver or call for zone may be an indicator of the power of the brand new fashion.

Challenges & Reminders:

Changing Environment:

The marketplace is dynamic, which means that that deliver and call for stages are situation to surprising fluctuations. Traders want to be on the lookout for signs and symptoms of a converting order float and adjust their evaluation to account for these circumstances.

2. Unreliable Indications:

Like any other technique, order float analysis is not wonderful. The potential for misguided indicators emphasizes how important chance management and validation with a number of signs are.

Chapter 3: Setting Up Your Trading Station

Choosing a broker and platform

Profitable investing requires you operate a brokerage service that aligns with your making an investment desires, educational desires and getting to know fashion. Especially for brand new buyers, deciding on the pleasant on line stock dealer that suits your desires can suggest the difference between an interesting new earnings movement and irritating sadness.

While there's no certain-fire way to guarantee investment returns, there's a manner to set yourself up for success through deciding on the on line brokerage that first-rate fits your needs. In this manual, we'll smash down everything you have to search for in your best brokerage, from the plain (like whether or not or not the platform lets in you to change the securities you're interested in) to the now not-so-apparent (like how clean it's far to get guide from an actual human while you want it).

Step 1: Know Your Needs

Before you begin clicking on brokerage ads, take a moment to hone in on what is maximum crucial to you in a trading platform. The solution will be barely extraordinary relying on your funding desires and where you are within the investment gaining knowledge of curve.

If you're simply starting out, you can prioritize capabilities like fundamental instructional assets, comprehensive glossaries, easy get entry to to support group of workers, and the capacity to area practice trades earlier than you begin gambling with actual cash.

If you've got a few funding experience already beneath your belt, but you're looking to get serious, you may need more excessive-level education and opinion-primarily based assets authored by professional traders and analysts, in addition to an awesome choice of fundamental and technical statistics.

A genuinely experienced investor, perhaps a person that's performed hundreds of trades already however is looking for a new brokerage, goes to prioritize superior charting competencies, conditional order alternatives, and the potential to alternate derivatives, mutual finances, commodities, and glued-earnings securities, in addition to stocks.

Be sincere with yourself approximately wherein you're right now on your investing adventure and in which you need to head. Are you seeking to establish a retirement fund and attention on passive investments that will generate tax-free income in an IRA or 401(k)? Do you need to attempt your hand at day-buying and selling but don't understand wherein to begin? Do you want the idea of tweaking and tailoring your personal portfolio, or are you willing to pay a professional to make certain it's performed right?

Depending on which course you need to observe, there can be many greater questions you'll need to answer alongside the way as you benefit experience and refine your dreams. For now, however, start with these four vital considerations that will help you decide which of the brokerage functions we discuss beneath will be most critical to you. To help get those analytical juices flowing, we've blanketed numerous sample questions underneath every broader subject matter:

Are You an Active or Passive Investor?

Do you need to be super hands-on and execute day or swing trades? Do you see yourself in the end leaving the nine-to-5 grind and turning into a full-time investor? Or, alternatively, do you want to discover a few strong investments to keep for the long haul with very little day-to-day interaction?

What Kind of Trades Do You Want to Execute?

Are you going to be the type of investor who is aware of what they need to do and just wishes a platform that makes it clean and short to execute trades, or do you want a broker with a broader range of sources to help you identify possibilities? What kind of securities are you centered on? Stocks, mutual finances, ETFs? If you're extra superior, do you furthermore may need to change alternatives, futures, and fixed-earnings securities? What approximately margin trading? Do you want access to conditional orders, prolonged-hours trading, and automated trading alternatives?

What Kind of Help Do You Want?

Do you want to move the DIY path, learn how to interpret charts and economic data to find and execute your own trades, or would you opt to lease a pro? If you need to do it yourself, in which are you at the learning curve? What form of resources will you want to further your understanding? Will you need easy get right of entry to assist personnel, or are you capable of examine what you want to understand via on line instructional sources? Are you satisfied to execute trades on-line, or will you need to name in to have a broking help you with the process?

What Are Your Investing Goals?

Why are you choosing to make investments? Are you looking to supplement your regular income to enhance your modern general of residing? Is there a selected event or expense you want to fund? Do you plan for this to in the end come to be your number one profits supply? Are you attempting to accumulate retirement financial savings and, in that case, do you already have a retirement account or will you need to open a brand new one with your selected brokerage?

There are no incorrect solutions to those questions. Be honest with yourself about how a lot time, energy, and attempt you're willing and capable of placed into your investments. Your solutions may also change through the years, and that's adequate. Don't try to expect all your wishes and goals for the relaxation of your lifestyles. Just begin with where you're proper now.

Step 2: Narrow the Field

Now which you have a clean idea of what your investment desires are and what basic services you'll look for in your ideal brokerage, it's time to whittle down your options a chunk. While there are sure brokerage capabilities as a way to be more vital for some buyers than for others, there are some matters any legitimate on-line brokerage need to have. With this sort of huge variety of available options, checking on these simple necessities is a super manner to slender the sphere quick.

Stock Broker Regulation and Trust

Is the Brokerage a Member of the Securities Investor Protection Corporation (SIPC)?

There will typically be some type of notation or disclaimer at the lowest of the home page. You can speedy appearance up the brokerage on the SIPC internet site.

Is the Brokerage a Member of the Financial Industry Regulatory Authority (FINRA)?

This need to also be very without a doubt noted in an smooth-to-discover place. You can look up brokerages on FINRA's Broker Check internet site.

Is the Brokerage Covered by using the Federal Deposit Insurance Corporation (FDIC)?

Investment merchandise—such as brokerage or retirement bills that put money into stocks, bonds, options, and annuities—are not FDIC insured, because the fee of investments cannot be guaranteed. If the brokerage offers CDs, Money Market Deposit Accounts (MMDAs), checking, or financial savings money owed, however, they should be completely backed by using the FDI

What Kind of Insurance Do They Provide to Protect You in Case the Company Fails?

As a member of the SIPC, the business enterprise must have insurance with a in keeping with-patron restrict of as a minimum $500,000, with $250,000 to be had for cash claims.2 If the business enterprise adheres to the Customer Protection Rule, it ought to also provide extra insurance above and beyond the simple requirements of the SIPC.

Is There Any Kind of Guarantee of Protection Against Fraud?

Will the company reimburse you for losses attributable to fraud? Make sure you double-test what the brokerage requires of you in order as a way to be reimbursed. Find out when you have to offer any documentation or take unique precautions to guard yourself.

What Are Current Customers Saying?

Try looking online for consumer opinions of the brokerage, using key phrases like "coverage declare," "fraud protection" and "customer service." Of route, on line reviews should typically be enthusiastic about a grain of salt – some people just like to complain. However, if there are numerous customers from specific sites all lodging the equal criticism then you can need to analyze further.

Online Security and Account Protection
It's crucial to recognize how nicely a brokerage facilitates you protect your facts.

Does the Brokerage Website Offer Two-Factor Authentication?

Do you have the choice of activating a safety feature similarly to your password? Common options can consist of answering security questions, receiving specific, time-sensitive codes thru text or email, or using a bodily security key that slots into your USB port.

What Kind of Technology Does the Broker Use to Keep Your Account Safe?

Find out if the broker uses encryption or "cookies," and if it definitely explains how it uses them to defend your account information and how they paintings.

Does the Company Ever Sell Customer Information to Third-Parties (like Advertisers)?

The solution must sincerely be no.

Brokerage Account Offerings

Since the forms of tools you want will depend on your desires, you ought to also do a short check for the following objects to weed out brokerages that virtually won't meet your desires.

What Kinds of Accounts Does the Broker Offer Besides Standard (Taxable) Investment Accounts?

For instance, if you have dependents, find out if you can open an Education Savings Account (ESA) or a custodial account in your toddler or different dependents.

Can You Open a Retirement Account?

Look into whether the broking offers Roth or traditional retirement money owed and if you could roll over an current 401k or IRA.

Are There Different Products for Different Investing Goals?

For instance, discover if the dealer offers managed money owed. Also, discover if there funding minimums for distinct varieties of debts.

Can You Manage Retirement Accounts for Employees Through the Brokerage?

This may additionally practice in case you're a small commercial enterprise proprietor. These varieties of debts consist of SIMPLE or SEP IRAs.

Does the Brokerage Offer Self-Directed IRAs or Solo 401k Options?

This applies if the best employee to your small business is you.

Step three: Figure Out the Fees

While there may be different things that rely extra to you than fees, you need to start out with a pretty clean concept of how a good deal you'll pay to apply any unique brokerage.

For some, a small top class may be justifiable if the platform offers functions that its less expensive competition lack. In preferred, however, you need to lose as little of your funding returns as viable to accounting expenses and buying and selling commissions.

By starting with the bottom line, you may without difficulty determine which stockbrokers are too steeply-priced to consider and which absolutely aren't well matched with the form of funding pastime you're focused on.

Broker Account Fees

Does the Broker Charge a Fee for Opening an Account?

Is There a Deposit Minimum?

Bear in thoughts that mutual finances often have funding minimums of $1,000 or greater, however that's not similar to a brokerage requiring that you deposit a minimal sum of money just to open an account.

Are There Any Annual or Monthly Account Maintenance Fees?

If so, are they waived for larger debts or is there an smooth manner to avoid them even in case your account balance is small?

Does the Broker Offer Access to a Trading Platform as Part of Their Free Membership?

If you're just starting out, the free platform may additionally fit your needs flawlessly.

Is There a Pro or Advanced Trading Platform That Is Pay-to-Play?

If you're a greater advanced investor, it's critical to know whether or not or not you'll want to pay to upgrade your account to get admission to equipment and resources which might be up on your velocity. Some superior systems are free for clients who agree to region a minimal wide variety of trades consistent with yr or make investments a minimal amount.

What Are the Margin Rates?

Margin buying and selling is handiest for extremely skilled investors who understand the dangers involved. If you're a new investor, this point receivers observe to you.

What's the Minimum Loan Amount and Account Balance?

Most brokerages will provide decrease interest rates for large amounts, however don't permit that be the cause you borrow more than you must.

Trading Commissions

Do Trading Commissions Depend on How Much You Have Invested Through the Brokerage or How Often You Trade?

For instance, some brokerages determine trading commissions primarily based at the account length, while others offer a discounted fee to clients who alternate a certain quantity in keeping with area.3

Make certain you look at the fees on the way to maximum probably observe to you based in your predicted account stability and buying and selling hobby.

Are There Different Commission Rates for Different Securities?

If you intend on trading more than shares, make sure you recognize what the costs are to exchange alternatives, bonds, futures, or different securities.

What Is the Minimum Investment for Mutual Funds or ETFs?

Make certain that mutual funds that allow you to shop for and sell free of charge (frequently known as No Transaction Fee, or NTF, finances) don't price other varieties of charges alternatively. Mutual price range often include a number of extraordinary forms of prices, a number of that may sneak up on you. Make certain you assessment the prospectus of any fund you're thinking about to make sure you recognize all the charges involved.

Does the Brokerage Offer Any Free or Reduced-Price Trades?

The range of 'bonus' trades you get hold of might also rely upon your account balance, so ensure you check on what's supplied for the account stage that might follow to you. Also, make certain to check on what forms of trades qualify for the cut price—if it is only for shares and if ETFs, alternatives, or fixed-earnings securities depend.

Is the Commission Schedule Conducive to the Kind of Trading You'd Be Doing?

Some brokerages increase their commission prices after a certain quantity of trades. If that is the case, clients that concentrate on passive, purchase-and-hold investing reap the maximum blessings.

Conversely, a few brokerages offer decreased commissions after a certain range of trades in any given quarter, so energetic traders are rewarded for the usage of the platform greater frequently.

If the Broker Offers Advisory Services, How Much Do They Cost?

If you're not looking to control your own portfolio for something cause, make certain you take note of consultant expenses very closely.

Step four: Test the Broker's Platform

While any brokerage should have a quite respectable description of what sorts of equipment and resources their trading platform offers, now and again the excellent way to assess platform best is to give it a check drive. For brokers that assist you to open an account without cost, it could even be well worth the effort to go through the signup system simply to access the trading platform if that's what's essential.

Whether the brokerage has a web-primarily based platform that all people can get entry to or a free downloadable platform that calls for no-strings signup, do what you could to get entry to the gear you'd sincerely use without spending a dime.

Even if you're a greater superior dealer, and there's no unfastened manner to play around with "Pro" tools, you may get a terrific concept of the pleasant of a brokerage's offerings simply through looking at its primary suite. If there's not anything in the standard platform that seems promising, it's not likely the advanced platform could be worth it slow both.

On the other hand, a few agencies offer a big array of equipment and sources with their free products, so don't write off brokerages with simplest one platform simply yet.

We've already spent an awesome amount of time narrowing down your alternatives primarily based on fee and primary account services. Now that we've sooner or later gotten to the amusing stuff, make sure you spend time searching on the functions available in more than one areas.

Go through the motions of putting a change to peer how easily the method operates. Pull up multiple quotes for shares and other securities, and click on every tab to peer what kind of records the platform affords. You have to also take a look at out any to be had screeners or other gear provided to help you discover investments that meet particular criteria.

Questions to Answer While Testing Platforms

What Types of Securities Can You Trade at the Platform?

You should already have dominated out any platforms that don't will let you change the securities you're interested by. Make sure this platform automatically lets in you to exchange preferred shares, IPOs, options, futures, or fixed-income securities. If you don't see unique protection on the platform, but you know that the brokerage helps it, strive searching to your account settings, or doing a quick search, to peer how you can activate those functions and study permission requirements.

Are Quotes in Real-Time? Are They Streaming?

There will be a couple of approaches you may pull up a rate quote for a given security, however no longer all of them will provide the most updated statistics. Make sure you're aware about in which you can find real-time streaming records to ensure your trades are properly-timed.

Vanguard's net-based totally platform, as an instance, provides actual-time statistics in its Ticker Profile pages, however it calls for guide fresh. Simple quote-stage information is delayed with the aid of 20 minutes or greater. Schwab's online charges also require guide refreshing, however the downloadable Street-smart Edge platform and its cloud-based totally counterpart both provide real-time streaming data.

Can You Set Up Customized Watch lists and Alerts?

If you're going to be a greater lively dealer, you'll in all likelihood want to be able to get hold of alert notifications thru text, further to e mail, and installation more than one watch lists based totally on unique standards.

Does the Platform Provide Screeners That You Can Customize to Find Stocks, ETFs, Mutual Funds, or Other Securities?

Even if you're state-of-the-art and have no concept what any of the alternatives certainly imply, play around with the diverse parameters to get an concept of the way smooth the tools are to apply. A precise platform can be intuitively prepared and clean to perform.

What Kinds of Orders Can You Place?

Go via the motions of setting a change and check what varieties of orders are provided. A fundamental platform has to provide at the least market, limit, stop, and forestall restrict. A higher platform will even assist you to vicinity trailing prevent orders, or market-on-close orders (which execute on the price the safety reaches at the marketplace last).

If you are trying to make surprisingly few trades, and you're now not interested in day or swing trading, a primary choice of order types has to be best. If you're trying to get into the nitty-gritty of inventory buying and selling, however, you have to search for a wider selection. If you're more superior, you must search for the capacity to region conditional orders that can help you set up multiple trades with particular triggers in order to execute routinely whilst your particular situations are met.

Do You Have Control Over Order Timing and Execution of Trades?

A simple platform has to at the least will let you area trades which might be exact-for-day (meaning they may be finished at any time during trading hours) or desirable-until-canceled (which keeps the order for as much as 60 days until it's far completed otherwise you cancel it).

A extra advanced platform will let you vicinity restriction orders with a few more variability, consisting of fill-or-kill (which robotically cancels the order if it isn't totally filled at once) or Immediate or cancel (which automatically cancels the order if it isn't at the least partially stuffed proper away).

Can You Trade in Extended Hours?

Stock and ETF trades take location outdoor of everyday market hours of 9:30 a.m. – 4 p.m. EST, the in pre-marketplace and after-hours durations. Each brokerage has its own definition of the particular time periods these Extended Hours classes occupy.

Not all systems assist you to change at some stage in extended hours, and a few only permit trading at some stage in after hours, but not throughout pre-marketplace hours. You can be charged a fee for extended hours trading, so ensure you review the phrases of those trades to make sure you aren't caught unawares.

Again, for brand new buyers, this selection might not be too critical. For extra advanced investors or folks who are seeking to be very lively, however, reviewing a brokerage's extended hours trading coverage is critical.

Charting Features

Now that you've played round with the platform a chunk, check the charting skills to explore the equipment at your disposal. Pay attention to what sorts of records you could plot, how easy it is to replace between charting technical research and reviewing fundamental or market facts, and what you could customize and store for later reference.

What Technical Indicators Are Available on the Chart?

In standard, the greater the higher. At the very least, you should be able to plot basic signs like extent, RSI, simple shifting averages, Bollinger bands, MACD, and stochastics. If any of those simple indicators are missing, it's time to transport on. You should additionally have the ability to plan at least a few company activities, like earnings reviews, stock splits, and dividend payments.

Can You Compare Different Stocks and Indices on the Same Chart?

Can you Draw at the Chart to Create Trend Lines, Free-form Diagrams, Fibonacci Circles, and Arcs, or Other Mark-Ups?

Does the Platform Have a Trading Journal or Other Means of Saving Your Work?

Whether you're mastering the way to examine charts or are a expert dealer who takes notes to maintain yourself heading in the right direction, having a manner to personalize and store your charts is a hugely beneficial tool. Related questions encompass:

In addition to creating fashion traces, are you able to draw on the chart absolutely to focus on important occasions so that you can take into account what to review later?

Can you shop your charts when you've custom designed them?

Can you make notes for later reference?

Can the ones notes be placed on the chart to make certain you understand what they follow to whilst you take a look at them later?

Other Options

Remember that a number of these options may also only be to be had on a Pro or Advanced platform. If you're an advanced lively trader, you'll probably want a broker that offers all of those options. If you're a more passive dealer, otherwise you're just no longer looking to pay a premium for bells and whistles you're not prepared for, sticking to a unfastened basic platform is just exceptional.

Can you automate trades through customized rules or imported algorithms?

Can the platform be custom designed to apprehend particular chart styles for expenses, signs, and oscillators?

Can you set up alerts to inform you while the platform finds a matching sample?

Does the Website or Platform Allow Paper Trading?

Paper buying and selling is a way for traders to exercise placing and executing trades without virtually the usage of cash. It's a notable manner for aspiring lively traders to practice and for buyers of all enjoy ranges to check out new techniques and hone their competencies without risking losses.

Does the Platform Allow Back testing?

Another manner to check out techniques and get snug with the manner earlier than placing cash on the road, back testing allows you to simulate a change primarily based on the historic performance of your selected security. It's a manner of putting a hypothetical, retroactive alternate after which seeing what would have took place had you done it in real existence.

Step 5: How Well Does the Stock Broker Educate Its Clients?
While a beneficial and useable trading platform is vital, you should also take some time to peruse the brokerage's academic offerings and try out the hunt feature.

If you're a new investor, you need on the way to search for phrases you don't know or locate advice on how to interpret records. If there's a subject you've been questioning approximately or a metric you don't completely apprehend, do a tribulation run using the quest characteristic and spot if you can discover the records you want quick and efficaciously.

Remember, what's intuitive and consumer-friendly for one investor may be a nightmarish maze of fruitless search queries for some other, so it's vital to find a platform that you may paintings with.

Once you've spent 20 minutes or so cruising a platform, you have to be capable of solution the following questions pretty without difficulty. If you couldn't, and a brief search of the web site for unique answers doesn't yield the vital facts, it's likely a sign that the brokerage's platform isn't always for you.

Stock Broker's Quality and Usability

All the academic resources in the world are vain if you couldn't access them without difficulty. A true platform or internet site have to offer a extensive range of instructional services, in a couple of mediums, to make certain customers are able to fast and easily find the records they want in a layout that works for their getting to know style. Before we dive into the precise styles of educational resources you should expect from a very good brokerage, allows first make sure the ones assets are person-pleasant.

What Types of Educational Offerings Does the Broker Provide?

Whether it gives motion pictures, podcasts, consumer forums, or written articles, the format needs to give you the results you want.

Where Does the Information Come from?

If the broker syndicates work from other sites, ensure the ones websites are authentic. If the web page has a weblog or other contributor content material, then make sure the contributing authors have enjoyed and authority you may consider.

How Easy and Intuitive Is the Site or Platform to Navigate?

Make certain getting from a research web page to the buying and selling display screen is a easy process. You do not need to feel like you're clicking in circles. Make sure special topics are smooth to locate at the website.

Does the Broker Offer Resources for Beginners?

These can include glossaries or how-to articles, essential analysis, portfolio diversification, a way to interpret technical research, and other newbie topics.

How Effective Is the Platform's Search Function?

You can determine this out by means of typing in a not unusual making an investment term or attempting to find topics you have questions about. How fast was the quest characteristic capable of retrieve the records you wanted? Was this fact immediately seen, or did you need to click via some pages to get to it?

Analytical Resources
Is There Ample Analysis for Each Security?
This ought to include analyst scores from a couple of resources, actual-time news items, and applicable market and sector statistics.

Is There Sufficient Fundamental Data Available?
Stock profiles, for instance, ought to encompass ancient facts for the issuing organization, like profits reviews, monetary statements (like cash flow, income statements, and stability sheets), dividend payments, inventory splits or buybacks, and SEC filings. There have to also be records about any insider buying and selling activity.

Is there marketplace facts for the U.S. And foreign markets? What approximately the industry and sector facts? How deeply are you capable of dive into the large-image situations surrounding marketplace performance?

Step 6: Ease of Depositing and Withdrawing Funds

Especially in case you're investing to complement your regular earnings, it's important to realize how smooth it is to transport money inside and outside of your brokerage account. If you're looking to appoint a extra set-it-and-overlook-it approach, being able to withdraw budget may not be as huge of a concern. Still, existence frequently throws us things we don't anticipate, so it's prudent to study the deposit, withdrawal, and funds agreement phrases of any brokerage you bear in mind.

Depositing Funds

How Can You Deposit Money into Your Brokerage Account?

Find out if you can deposit finances thru take a look at, ACH transfer, twine, or credit score card (this isn't always encouraged, however it may nonetheless be an alternative).

Make sure you verify whether or not or not there are any expenses related to these options – even though most brokerages don't charge for deposits.

How Long Does It Take for Deposited Funds to Settle?

If you've spotted a notable change access however you don't have sufficient coins in your account to execute it, settling times will all of sudden become very important. Verify what number of days it takes for deposited finances to be to be had for funding.

Settlement instances may range depending on the supply of the deposit. Note that you may see longer settlement instances in case you hold a low stability or don't change very often.

Does the Brokerage Offer Regular Checking or Savings Accounts That Can Facilitate Swifter Transfers?

If the brokerage gives regular checking and savings accounts which are unfastened (and FDIC insured), it might be easier to go away funds in a linked banking account so they may be moved more quickly in your brokerage account if and while you want to bulk up your funding account.

Withdrawing Funds

How Long Does It Take Funds from the Sale of Your Investments to Settle?

Make sure you check on agreement instances for the one-of-a-kind forms of securities you will be buying and selling.

What About Dividend or Interest Distributions?

How quickly are those finances to be had for funding? For withdrawal?

How Easy Is It to Withdraw Funds From Your Brokerage Account?

Find out if you could withdraw thru ACH transfer, cord, or test and the way long it will take for those price range to reach your financial institution account. Also, test to discover if there's a fee for withdrawal.

Does the brokerage offer the choice of a debit or ATM card attached for your account? Sometimes this is supplied for a brokerage account, and other times you want to open a linked checking or savings account to access this option. If you do have the option of a card, find out which ATMs can you use and if there are any charges associated with card use.

Step 7: Customer Service

By now, you've possibly narrowed your alternatives to one or two brokerages that without a doubt blow you away in terms of resources, features, and usability. Whether you've determined your ideal platform or you're still at the fence, take just a few greater mines to peruse the Help phase of the brokerages you're considering.

If you're a new investor and also you're feeling crushed, ensure you could get in touch with the service workforce quickly and effortlessly. If you're technically challenged, make certain the tech aid group is simple to contact and to be had round the clock.

While these gadgets receiver's make or damage your brokerage choice, it's nonetheless critical to make sure you understand a way to get help while and if you want it.

Is there a dedicated range you may name to speak to a human for change help?

Make certain you are aware about any extra fees for name-assisted trades.

Is there an automatic quantity you can call for fundamental queries?

What about fashionable assist? What are the call-in hours for representative help?

What are the hours of operation for phone lines? Can you name 24/7, or are the phones only staffed in the course of ordinary business hours?

For individuals who are interaction averse, is there an e mail deal with you may use to get hold of prompt assistance?

Does the brokerage use a stable inner messaging machine for crucial files and account queries?

Does the website have an online chat alternative for fast assistance?

What when you have a fundamental query however don't need to Trojan horse a representative? Is there a searchable FAQ phase that answers a huge range of questions?

What approximately tech support? Are there dedicated telephone traces, electronic mail addresses, or chat structures for gaining access to technical help?

Step 8: Get Going and Next Steps

We know it could be tempting to simply sign up for whichever brokerage has the maximum competitive advert marketing campaign, but a hit making an investment requires attention to element long earlier than you vicinity your first change.

If you're seeking to make trading a protracted-time period hobby, a destiny profession, or just a approach of bulking up your retirement fund, then it's important which you use the gear and assets in order to set you up for a successful and exciting revel in.

By following this in-intensity guide, you've optimistically observed the platform in order to excellent serve your desires, whatever they might be. You can locate assist sorting through the exceptional agents on our stock broking opinions web page.

Once you've singled out your excellent brokerage, it's time to get commenced. Don't just installation an account and pass on to the following aspect. Really dive in. Use the educational and research resources to be had to you, start outlining your funding approach, and make the maximum of all the equipment at your disposal.

You've spent precious time identifying which features count most to you—now it's time to put them to work.

Join 120 million registered customers exchanging the Purchase and exchange Whether you are a novice dealer, crypto fanatic, or expert, you'll gain from access to the global crypto markets even as taking part in some of the Plus, tools and guides that make it easy to at the Finance app.

Setting up charts and indicators

Setting up charts and signs starts off evolved with deciding on a dependable buying and selling platform that gives sturdy charting equipment and giant customization alternatives. A suitable platform must provide real-time records, a number of chart kinds, and a wide range of technical indicators. Popular buying and selling platforms like MetaTrader, Trading View, and Thinkorswim are favored by way of investors for their user-pleasant interfaces and superior analytical abilities. Ensuring the platform meets your buying and selling wishes is crucial for effective chart setup.

Choosing the Chart Type

Once the trading platform is chosen, the subsequent step is to pick out the suitable chart type. Different chart kinds can offer numerous views on fee moves. Candlestick charts are extensively used amongst day investors due to the fact they offer a complete view of the market, showing the outlet, closing, high, and occasional fees for every time period. Bar charts and line charts also are useful, but they won't offer the same level of element as candlestick charts. Selecting the proper chart type is crucial for accurate marketplace analysis.

Customizing the Time Frame

Customizing the chart's time body is crucial for capturing applicable marketplace statistics. Day buyers often attention on shorter time frames, which include one-minute, 5-minute, or fifteen-minute charts, to investigate intraday rate moves. Adjusting the timeframe lets in investors to zoom in on unique durations and become aware of patterns and traits which might be pertinent to their trading strategies. The preference of time frame should align with the trader's goals and trading style.

Adding and Configuring Indicators

Indicators are crucial equipment for technical evaluation, assisting buyers interpret price actions and become aware of buying and selling opportunities. Common indicators consist of moving averages, Relative Strength Index (RSI), Bollinger Bands, and MACD (Moving Average Convergence Divergence). Each indicator serves a distinct reason:

Moving Averages: Smooth out charge data to assist become aware of the course of the fashion.
RSI: Measures the rate and alternate of price actions to decide overbought or oversold situations.
Bollinger Bands: Highlight volatility and capacity reversal points.
MACD: Combines shifting averages to show modifications in momentum.
Traders need to configure those indicators in keeping with their particular techniques and market conditions. This would possibly contain adjusting the duration

settings or combining a couple of indicators to verify signals.

Interpreting Indicators

Understanding a way to interpret signs is critical for making knowledgeable buying and selling decisions. For example, a transferring common crossover would possibly sign a capability trend reversal, whilst an RSI studying above 70 should suggest overbought situations. Traders often use a combination of indicators to growth the reliability of their analysis. Learning to read these indicators appropriately can drastically beautify a trader's capacity to assume marketplace movements.

Regular Monitoring and Adjustment

Market conditions are dynamic, and what works in one scenario won't be powerful in some other. Therefore, continuous monitoring and adjustment of chart setups and indicator configurations are important. Traders ought to frequently evaluation their settings to make sure they remain aligned with cutting-edge marketplace trends and situations. This iterative procedure helps buyers stay adaptable and responsive, optimizing their strategies for better performance.

Mastering Chart Setup and Indicator Use

Setting up charts and signs is a skill that calls for practice and enjoy. By gaining knowledge of this issue of buying and selling, investors can benefit a deeper understanding of marketplace behavior, improve their buying and selling accuracy, and decorate their ability to seize profitable possibilities. Consistent refinement and version of chart setups and indicator parameters are key to retaining a aggressive edge in the speedy-paced world of day buying and selling.

Configuring trading software

Configuring buying and selling software program starts off evolved with choosing the ideal platform that aligns with your buying and selling desires. Popular choices together with MetaTrader, Trading View, and Thinkorswim provide various capabilities suitable to each newbie and experienced traders. When deciding on buying and selling software program, recollect factors consisting of ease of use, the provision of technical analysis equipment, actual-time statistics get right of entry to, and the ability to execute trades quick. The right software has to provide a stability between complete capability and user-pleasant layout to make certain green trading operations.

Setting Up User Preferences

Once the buying and selling software is chosen, putting in person possibilities is the subsequent step. This includes configuring the software program's interface to healthy your trading fashion and choices. Customize the dashboard to display applicable records which include watch lists, buying and selling signals, information feeds, and marketplace summaries. Personalizing those elements allows streamline the trading technique, allowing you to get admission to crucial statistics fast and make knowledgeable choices without navigating thru needless litter.

Integrating Data Feeds and News Sources

Integrating information feeds and information sources into your trading software program is vital for staying up to date on market conditions and events that may influence fee actions. Reliable and actual-time facts feeds provide the trendy marketplace fees, volumes, and trends, which can be essential for correct evaluation and well timed trading. Incorporate trusted information resources that offer insights and updates on economic signs, company income, geopolitical occasions, and other factors that affect the markets. Keeping abreast of real-time records permit you to anticipate market actions and alter your strategies therefore.

Configuring Technical Indicators and Tools

Trading software frequently comes prepared with quite a few technical signs and tools that useful resource in market evaluation. Configuring those equipment involves selecting signs that align together with your trading method and putting their parameters to optimize performance. Common technical indicators consist of shifting averages, MACD, RSI, and Fibonacci retracement stages. Setting up those signs includes deciding on the appropriate time frames, adjusting sensitivity settings, and mixing more than one indicators to generate dependable alerts. Proper configuration complements your potential to identify tendencies, reversals, and potential entry and go out points.

Implementing Risk Management Settings

Effective chance management is a cornerstone of a success trading. Configuring threat management settings inside your buying and selling software program enables protect your investments and mitigate capability losses. Set up forestall-loss and take-profit orders to mechanically close trades at predetermined tiers, thereby restricting losses and securing income. Additionally, establish function sizing rules to ensure that you do no longer overexpose your account to any single alternate. By integrating these danger control gear into your buying and selling software program, you could preserve a disciplined approach and shield your capital.

Automating Trading Strategies

Many advanced buying and selling software platforms offer functions that allow for the automation of trading strategies. Configuring automatic trading includes programming your techniques into the software, placing standards for trade execution, and establishing parameters for access and exit factors. Automated trading can decorate performance through executing trades based totally on predefined guidelines, minimizing the emotional effect of trading choices. Ensure that your automatic strategies are very well examined and optimized to perform beneath various marketplace situations before deploying them in a live buying and selling environment.

Continuous Monitoring and Updating

The configuration of trading software isn't always a one-time undertaking; it requires non-stop tracking and updating to adapt to changing marketplace situations and private trading desires. Regularly overview your software program settings, consumer choices, and the performance of your technical indicators. Stay up to date with software program updates and new functions that may beautify your buying and selling talents. By maintaining a proactive approach to software configuration, you may make certain that your trading equipment remain effective and aligned along with your evolving buying and selling strategies.

Mastering Trading Software Configuration

Mastering the configuration of buying and selling software program is essential for maximizing its ability and attaining buying and selling achievement. By cautiously selecting the right platform, setting up person possibilities, integrating facts feeds, configuring technical indicators, implementing chance management settings, automating strategies, and continuously monitoring your setup, you could create a effective buying and selling environment tailored for your desires. This meticulous technique to configuring trading software will beautify your analytical abilities, enhance change execution, and in the long run make contributions to better trading outcon.

Chapter 4: Chart Patterns

Chart styles are important equipment in technical evaluation, utilized by investors to are expecting destiny fee movements based on ancient price statistics. These styles shape on fee charts and sign potential marketplace developments, whether or not they are persevering with or reversing. Understanding and figuring out those styles can help buyers make knowledgeable selections and expand effective buying and selling techniques.

Reversal patterns

A reversal is a exchange inside the fee path of an asset. A reversal can occur to the upside or disadvantage. Following an uptrend, a reversal would be to the drawback. Following a downtrend, a reversal might be to the upside. Reversals are primarily based on average price course and are not commonly based on one or two periods/bars on a chart.

Certain signs, any such shifting common, oscillator, or channel, may additionally assist in setting apart trends in addition to recognizing reversals. Reversals can be in comparison with breakouts.

What Does a Reversal Tell You?

Reversals regularly occur in intraday buying and selling and take place rather speedy, but they also occur over days, weeks, and years. Reversals arise in exceptional time frames which might be applicable to different investors. An intraday reversal on a 5-minute chart doesn't remember to a protracted-term investor who's looking for a reversal on each day or weekly charts. Yet, the 5-minute reversal may be very important to a day dealer.

An uptrend, that's a sequence of better swing highs and better lows, reverses into a downtrend through converting to a sequence of lower highs and decrease lows. A downtrend, that's a series of decrease highs and lower lows, reverses into an uptrend by way of changing to a series of higher highs and better lows.

Trends and reversals may be diagnosed primarily based on charge motion on my own, as defined above, or different investors choose using indicators. Moving averages can also resource in spotting both the fashion and reversals. If the fee is above a growing moving average then the trend is up, but while the charge drops underneath the moving average that might sign a ability charge reversal.

Trend lines also are used to spot reversals. Since an uptrend makes higher lows, a trend line can be drawn along the ones higher lows. When the price drops below the trend line, that could suggest a trend reversal.

If reversals were clean to identify, and to distinguish from noise or short pullbacks, buying and selling would be smooth. But it isn't always. Whether the usage of price movement or signs, many fake indicators occur and sometimes reversals show up so quick that buyers are not capable of act quickly sufficient to avoid a large loss.

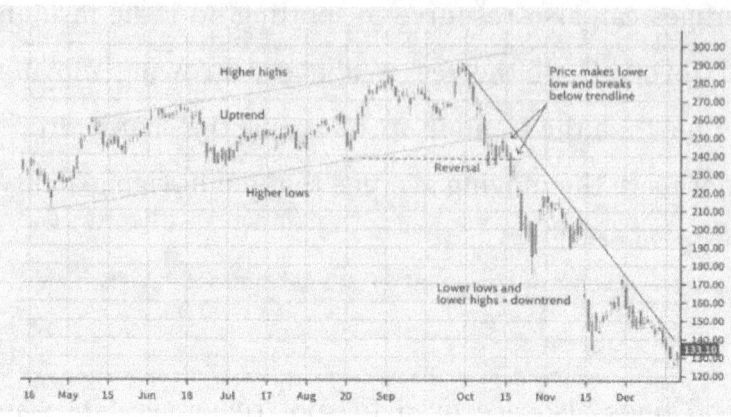

The chart shows an uptrend shifting with a channel, making normal higher highs and higher lows. The rate first breaks out of the channel and under the trend line, signaling a probable fashion exchange. The price then additionally makes a lower low, losing underneath the prior low in the channel. This in addition confirms the reversal to the disadvantage.

The charge then continues decrease, making decrease lows and lower highs. A reversal to the upside might not arise until the fee makes a higher excessive and higher low. A circulate above the descending trend line, although, may want to difficulty an early caution signal of a reversal.

Continuation patterns

When a trader seems on the price chart of a inventory, it may appear like absolutely random moves. This is regularly true and, yet, within the ones price movements are patterns. Chart styles are geometric shapes found in the charge facts that could help a dealer understand the charge motion, as well as make predictions about wherein the price is possibly to go.

Traders regularly count on that an occurrence of a continuation pattern suggests that a rate fashion is likely to hold, however skilled buyers accept the concept that no sample is perfectly reliable for predictive purposes. This article provides an introduction to continuation styles, explaining what these patterns are and a way to spot them.

Varieties of Continuation Patterns

Continuation styles occur mid-fashion and are a pause inside the charge motion of varying durations. When those styles occur, it is able to imply that the trend is possibly to renew after the sample completes. A sample is taken into consideration entire when the pattern has formed (may be drawn) and then "breaks out" of that pattern, probably continuing on with the former fashion. Continuation styles can be visible on all time frames, from a tick chart to a every day or weekly chart. Common continuation patterns encompass triangles, flags, pennants, and rectangles

Triangles

Triangles are a commonplace pattern and can truly be defined as a converging of the rate range, with better lows and lower highs. The converging rate motion creates a triangle formation. There are 3 fundamental sorts of triangles: symmetrical, ascending and descending. For buying and selling functions, the 3 kinds of triangles can be traded similarly. Triangles vary of their period but may have at the least swing highs in charge and swings lows in charge. As price keeps to converge, it'll subsequently attain the apex of the triangle; the toward the apex fee receives, the tighter and tighter rate movement will become, hence creating a breakout extra approaching.

Symmetrical: A symmetrical triangle can be genuinely defined as a downward sloping higher bound and an upward sloping lower sure in charge.

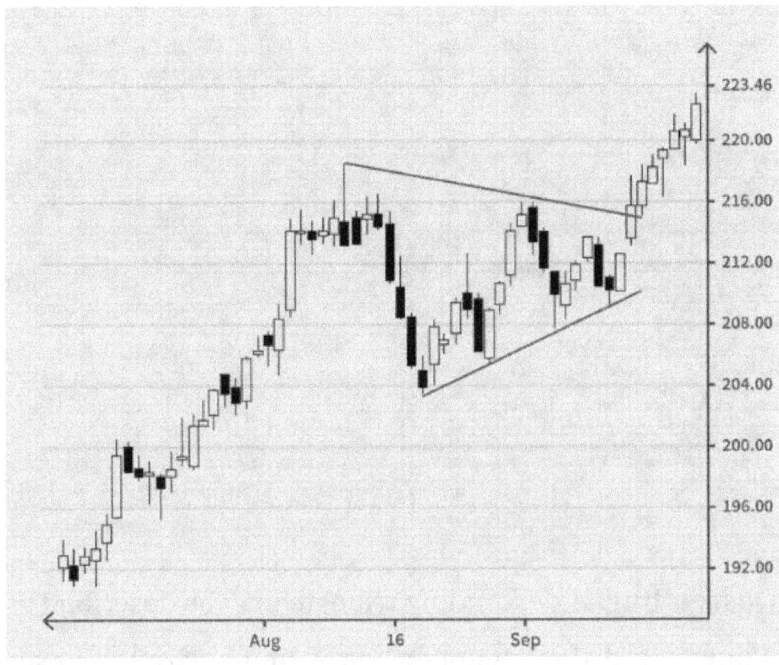

Ascending: An ascending triangle can be described as a horizontal higher certain and upward sloping decrease sure.

Descending: A descending triangle may be described as a downward sloping upper bound and horizontal lower bound.

Flags

Flags are a pause inside the trend, in which the price will become confined in a small fee range between parallel strains. This pause inside the center of a fashion offers the pattern a flag-like look. Flags are normally quick in duration, lasting numerous bars, and do now not contain fee swings backward and forward as a buying and selling variety or trend channel might. Flags can be parallel or upward or downward sloping, as shown in beneath.

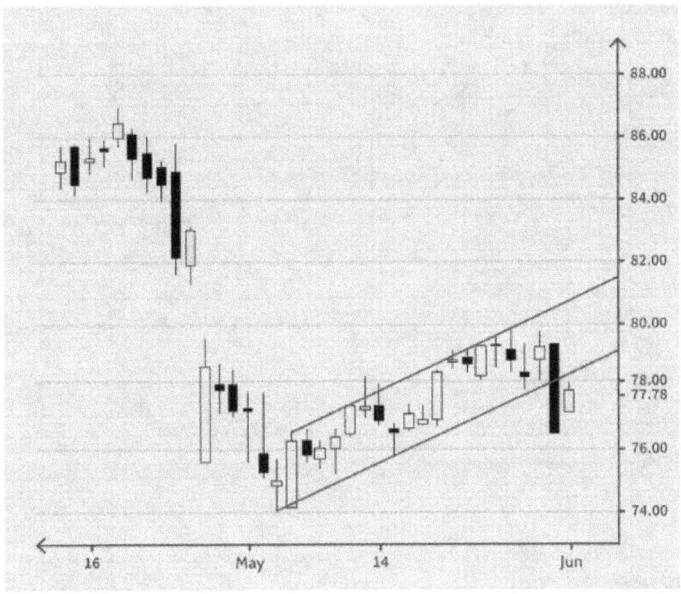

Pennants

Pennants are just like a triangle, yet smaller; pennants are usually created by using best several bars. While now not a hard and speedy rule, if a pennant consists of greater than 20 rate bars, it is able to be taken into consideration a triangle. The pattern is created as costs converge, protecting a extraordinarily small charge range mid-trend; this gives the sample a pennant look.

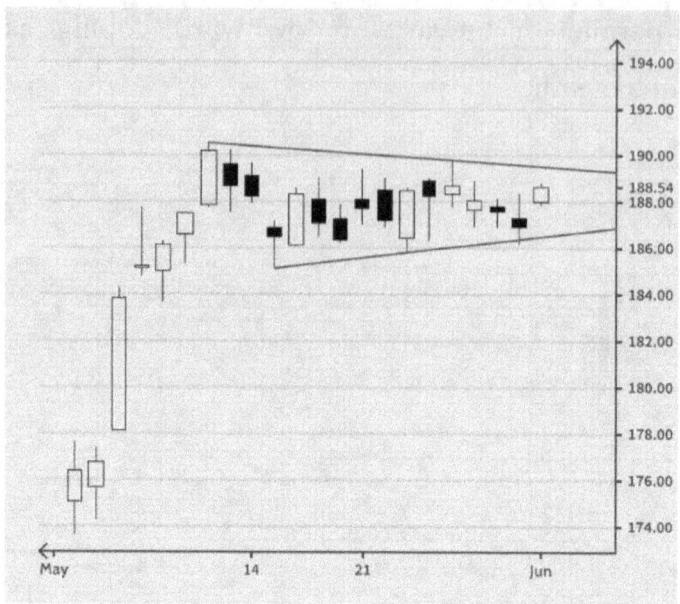

Rectangles

Often there may be pauses in a trend in which the rate action movements sideways, certain among parallel support and resistance strains. Rectangles, additionally known as trading degrees, can closing for brief intervals or many years. This sample is very commonplace and may be visible often intra-day, in addition to on longer-term time frames.

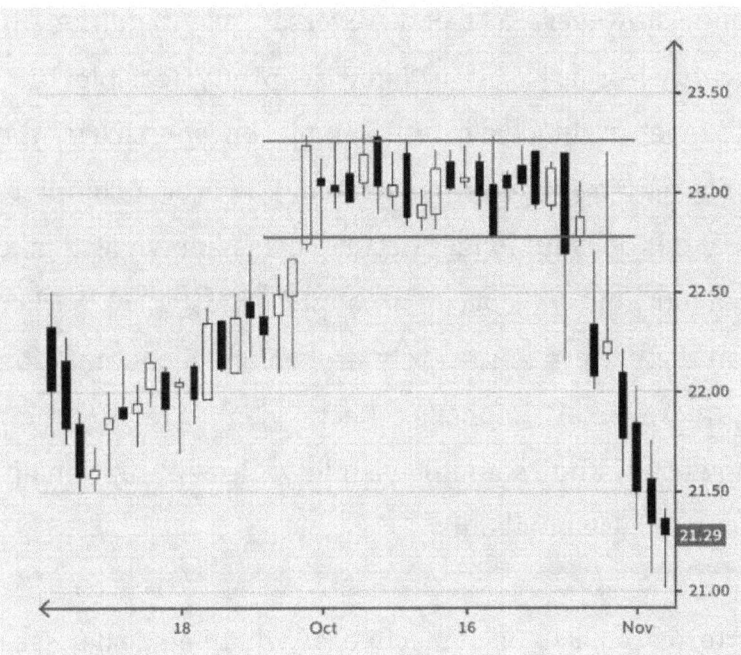

Working with Continuation Patterns

Continuation styles offer some good judgment to the charge action. By understanding the patterns, a dealer can create a trading plan to take benefit of common patterns. The styles gift buying and selling opportunities that may not be visible the usage of other methods.

Unfortunately, sincerely because the pattern is known as a "continuation pattern" does now not imply it's far always reliable. A sample may also appear throughout a trend; however, a trend reversal may additionally nevertheless arise. It is likewise pretty feasible that, once we've got drawn the sample on our charts, the limits may be slightly penetrated, however a complete breakout does no longer occur. This is known as a fake breakout and will occur a couple of instances earlier than the pattern is sincerely broken and a continuation or a reversal happens. Rectangles, due to their popularity and smooth visibility, are exceptionally prone to false breakouts.

Patterns can also be subjective, as what one dealer sees isn't always what every other trader sees, or how some other trader could draw or outline the sample in actual time. This is not necessarily a terrible element, as it could offer investors with a unique perspective on the market. It would require time and practice for the dealer to increase his or her skill in locating styles, drawing them and formulating a plan on the way to use them.

Breakout patterns

A breakout refers to when the fee of an asset moves above a resistance location, or actions below a guide area. Breakouts imply the ability for the fee to begin trending within the breakout route. For example, a breakout to the upside from a chart pattern may want to indicate the rate will begin trending higher. Breakouts that occur on high volume (relative to normal quantity) display more conviction this means that the price is much more likely to fashion in that path.

What Does a Breakout Tell You?

A breakout takes place because the rate has been contained underneath a resistance degree or above a guide degree, probably for some time. The resistance or help stage becomes a line inside the sand which many traders use to set access points or forestall loss degrees. When the fee breaks via the help or resistance level traders awaiting the breakout bounce in, and those who failed to need the fee to breakout go out their positions to keep away from larger losses.

This flurry of hobby will regularly reason extent to rise, which shows plenty of buyers have been interested in the breakout stage. The better than common volume helps affirm the breakout. If there's little extent at the breakout, the extent won't have been full-size to a whole lot of buyers, or now not sufficient investors felt convicted to location a trade close to the extent yet. These low extent breakouts are much more likely to fail. In the case of an upside breakout, if it fails the rate will fall back underneath resistance. In the case of a downside breakout, frequently known as a breakdown, if it fails the fee will rally returned above the assist stage it broke under.

Breakouts are generally associated with levels or other chart patterns, inclusive of triangles, flags, wedges, and head-and-shoulders. These styles are fashioned when the price actions in a particular way which leads to properly-described guide and/or resistance levels. Traders then watch these stages for breakouts. They can also initiate long positions or exit brief positions if the fee breaks above resistance, or they'll initiate quick positions or go out lengthy role if the price breaks underneath guide.

Even after a high volume breakout, the fee will regularly (but no longer constantly) retrace to the breakout factor before transferring inside the breakout route once more. This is because short-term investors will regularly purchase the initial breakout, but then try and sell quite speedy for a earnings. This promoting temporarily drives the fee again to the breakout point. If the breakout is valid (no longer a failure), then the rate should move back inside the breakout route. If it does not, it's a failed breakout.

Traders who use breakouts to provoke trades generally make use of prevent-loss orders in case the breakout fails. In the case of going lengthy on an upside breakout, a prevent loss is normally positioned just beneath the resistance degree. In the case of going short on a drawback breakout, a stop loss is usually placed simply above the assist stage that has been breached.

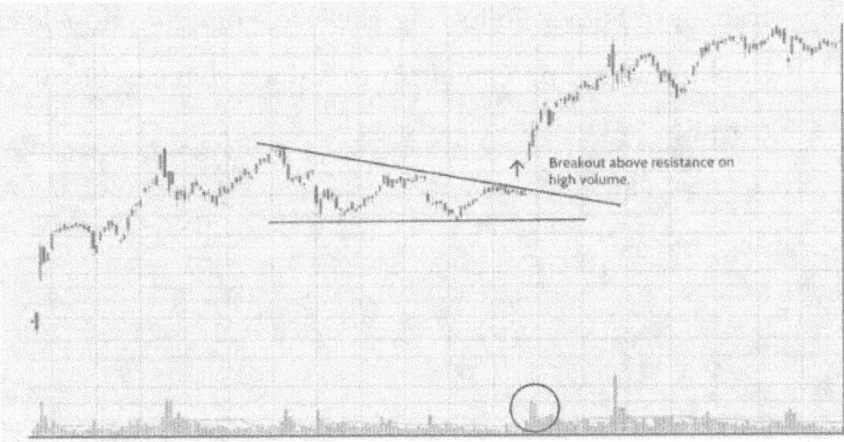

The chart shows a huge increase in extent, associated with an earnings launch, as the price breaks through the resistance place of a triangle chart sample. The breakout turned into so robust that it brought on a price gap. The charge persisted to move higher and didn't retrace to the original breakout point. That is an indication of a very strong breakout.

Traders may want to have used the breakout to potentially enter lengthy positions and/or get out of brief positions. If entering long, a forestall loss could be positioned simply below the resistance degree of the triangle (or maybe under triangle help). Because the charge had a huge gaping breakout, this prevent loss vicinity might not be ideal. After the rate persevered to transport higher following the breakout the stop loss can be trailed up in an effort to reduce chance or lock in a profit.

Chapter 5: Technical Indicators

Trend investors attempt to isolate and extract benefit from traits. The method of trend trading tries to capture profits thru the analysis of an asset's momentum in a specific path. This may be finished in a couple of ways.

No single technical indicator will punch your price ticket to market riches. Traders should additionally be well-versed in chance management and buying and selling psychology in addition to analysis. But certain techniques have stood the check of time and stay popular equipment for trend buyers who're interested in analyzing certain marketplace indicators.

Moving Averages

Moving average is a technical analysis device that smooths out rate records via creating a continuously up to date average rate. A transferring average creates a single, flat line on a price chart that successfully eliminates any variations due to random rate fluctuations.

The average is taken over a selected period: 10 days, 20 mins, 30 weeks, or any time the trader chooses. The 2 hundred-day, a hundred-day, and 50-day easy shifting common are famous alternatives for traders and long-time period trend followers.

The shifting average may be used in numerous approaches. The first is to take a look at the attitude of the moving common. The rate is not trending however ranging if it's mostly moving horizontally for an extended time. A trading range happens while a safety trades among constant excessive and occasional expenses for a period which includes days, weeks, or months. Many traders use techniques that follow those trading styles.

An uptrend is underway if the moving common line is angled up but transferring averages don't make predictions about the destiny cost of a inventory. They clearly reveal what the rate is doing on common over a time frame.

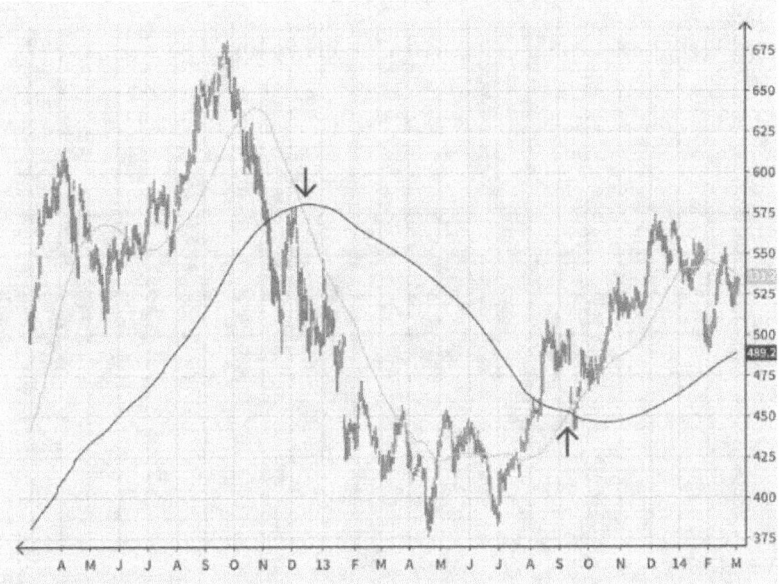

It also can be used as a buy signal whilst the charge crosses above a transferring common and it may be used as a promote signal when the rate crosses underneath a transferring average. But this technique is liable to greater fake alerts due to the fact the fee is greater risky than the moving common.

Moving averages also can offer help or resistance to the charge This chart indicates a 100-day transferring common acting as aid. The rate bounces off it.

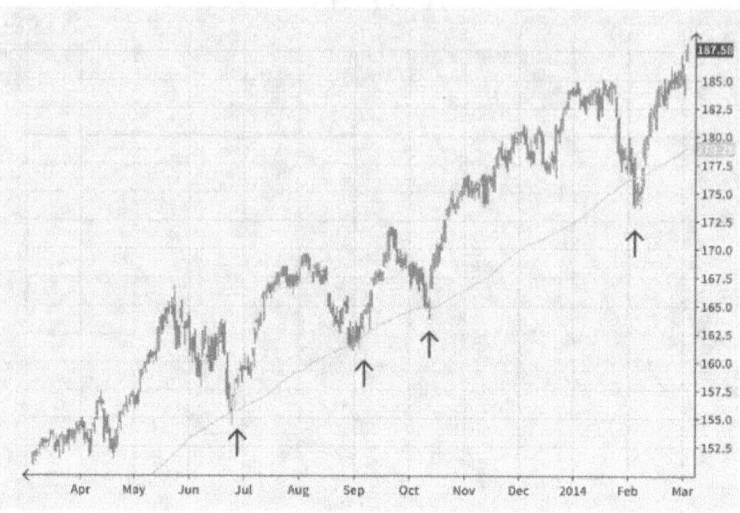

Moving Average Convergence Divergence (MACD)

The moving average convergence divergence (MACD) is a kind of oscillating indicator. One simple MACD approach is to study which aspect of zero the MACD traces are on in the histogram beneath the chart.

The inventory is possibly trending upward if the MACD strains are above zero for a sustained length. The fashion is in all likelihood downward if the MACD strains are below 0 for a sustained period. Potential purchase alerts arise using this strategy whilst the MACD movements above 0. Potential sell indicators occur whilst it crosses beneath zero. Signal line crossovers can also offer additional buy and sell signals. A MACD has strains: a fast line and a sluggish line.

A purchase signal occurs whilst the fast line crosses through and above the gradual line. A promote signal occurs while the fast line crosses via and underneath the gradual line.

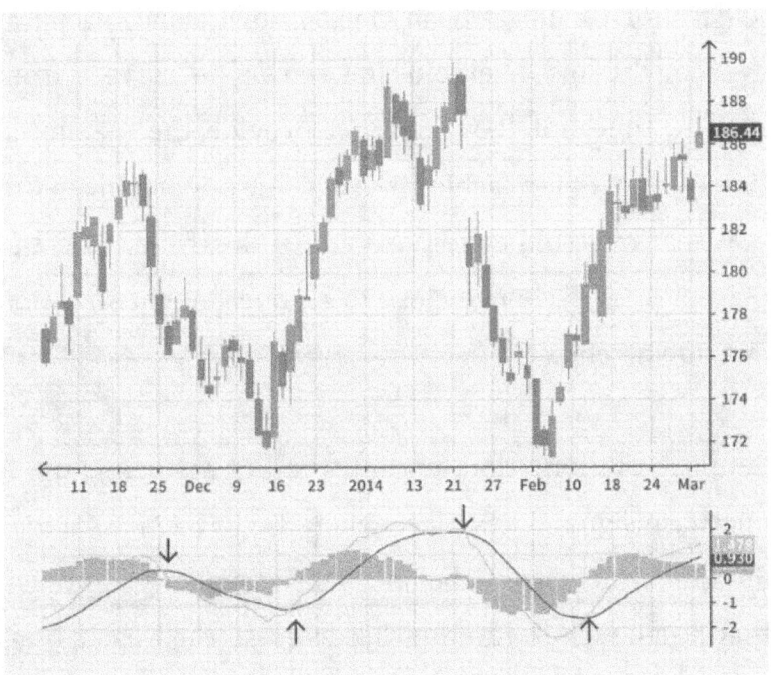

Relative Strength Index (RSI)

The relative power index (RSI) is any other oscillating indicator but its movement is contained between zero and a hundred so it affords specific records than the MACD.

The rate will often attain 70 and above for sustained intervals in a robust uptrend. The fee can stay at 30 or under for a long term in a downtrend. General overbought and oversold stages can be correct from time to time but they may not provide the maximum timely signals for fashion buyers. An opportunity is to buy near oversold conditions whilst the trend is up and place a brief exchange close to an overbought situation in a downtrend.

Suppose the long-time period trend of a stock is up. A purchase signal takes place when the RSI actions under 50 after which again above it. This essentially approach that a pullback in rate has occurred so the dealer buys when the pullback appears to have ended in step with the RSI and the fashion is resuming.

The 50 tiers are used because the RSI does not typically attain 30 in an uptrend except a capability reversal is underway. A quick-exchange signal happens when the fashion is down and the RSI actions above 50 after which lower back below it. Trendlines or a moving common can help establish the trend path and wherein direction to take exchange alerts.

On-Balance Volume (OBV)

Volume itself is a valuable indicator and on-balance volume (OBV) takes a good sized amount of quantity records and compiles it into a unmarried one-line indicator. The indicator measures cumulative buying and selling strain by way of including the quantity on "up" days and subtracting volume on "down" days. The volume must ideally confirm tendencies. A growing fee need to be accompanied by using a rising OBV. A falling fee should be followed by way of a falling OBV This figure indicates the shares of Netflix Inc. (NFLX) trending higher alongside OBV. It changed into a great indication that the charge changed into likely to preserve trending better even after the pullbacks due to the fact OBV didn't drop underneath its trend line.

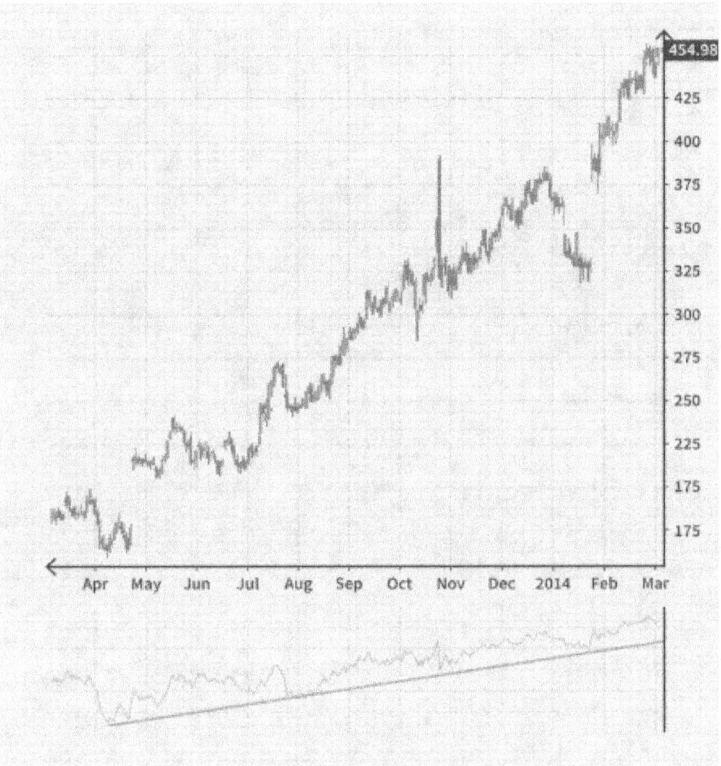

The rate will likely comply with the OBV inside the future and start rising if OBV is growing and the charge isn't. The rate may be near a pinnacle if it's growing and the OBV is flat-lining or falling. The charge might be nearing a bottom if it's falling and OBV is flat-lining or growing.

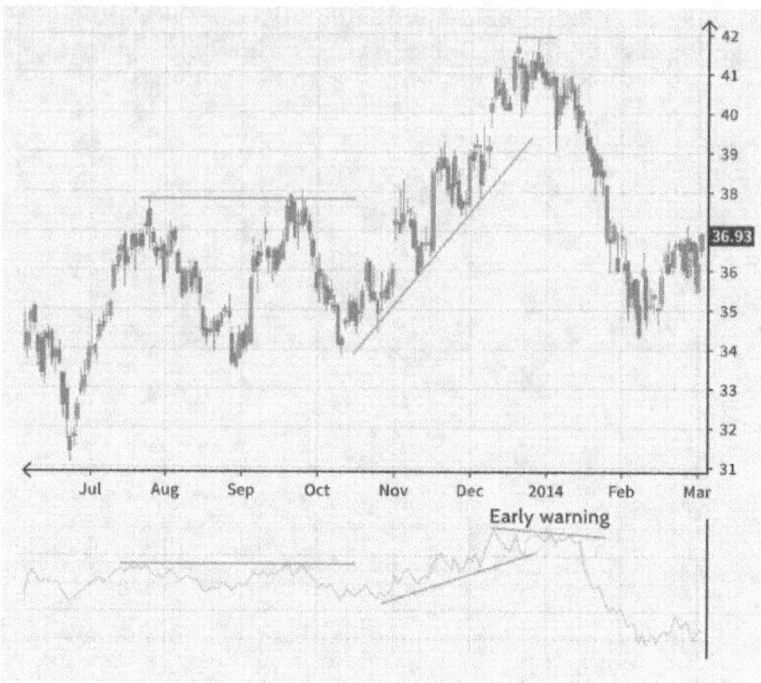

What Is an Oscillating Indicator?

An oscillating indicator is a technical evaluation indicator that varies through the years inside a band above and beneath a centerline. The MACD is an oscillating indicator that fluctuates above and below zero. It's both a fashion-following and a momentum indicator.

Momentum indicators

Momentum indicators are equipment utilized by traders to get a better know-how of the rate or fee at which the fee of a safety modifications. Momentum signs are first-class used with different signs and equipment due to the fact they don't work to perceive the path of motion, best the time-frame wherein the fee trade is happening.

Advantages of Momentum Indicators

Momentum indicators display the motion of charge over time and how robust those moves are/may be, regardless of the course the fee actions, up, or down.

Momentum indicators also are especially useful, as they help investors and analysts spot points in which the market can and could reverse. The points are identified thru divergence among charge motion and momentum.

Because momentum indicators show the relative electricity of fee movements however omit the directionality of the fee movements, such signs are first-class applied in aggregate with different technical signs

– consisting of fashion strains and shifting averages – which show price tendencies and guidelines.

Understanding Divergence

Divergence occurs while, for instance, the fee of a inventory is continually moving downward, following along side the momentum indicator getting used (which alerts sturdy momentum), but then the momentum indicator turns to the upside or not maintains to comply with the downward fee motion. It method that the indicator's diverged from the rate motion and indicates that the momentum of the contemporary rate movement is failing.

The chart under indicates how the Relative Strength Index (RSI) momentum indicator exhibits forthcoming rate course modifications as the motion of the RSI diverges from the course of price motion within the AUD/USD forex pair.

Divergence is normally a demonstration that the modern-day price fashion – due to the sign that momentum is stalling – is probably coming to an cease and is about to opposite. When price movement and momentum diverge in an upward style, it is a bullish divergence. If fee movement and the momentum indicator had been always shifting upward and the momentum indicator all at once became to the disadvantage, it'd be a bearish divergence.

Popular Momentum Indicators

There are a number of momentum indicators that investors can utilize. However, there are some which can be very famous with buyers and widely used.

1. Moving Average Convergence Divergence (MACD)

The Moving Average Convergence Divergence (MACD) is one of the most popular momentum signs. The MACD makes use of two indicators – shifting averages – turning them into an oscillator by using taking the longer average out of the shorter average. It means that the MACD suggests momentum because it oscillates among transferring averages as they converge, overlap, and move far from one another.

As stated above, the MACD uses two transferring averages. While it's miles up to the discretion of the dealer or analyst, the indicator usually makes use of the

12-day and 26-day exponential transferring averages (EMAs), subtracting the 26-day from the 12-day. The end result is the MACD line, that's then typically graphed with a 9-day EMA, appearing as a signal line that could pick out charge movement turns.

The without a doubt crucial aspect of the MACD is the histogram, which famous the difference among the MACD line and the 9-day EMA. When the histogram is tremendous – over the 0-midpoint line but starts to fall closer to the midline – it indicators a weakening uptrend. On the flipside, when the histogram is bad, under the 0-midpoint line however begins to climb toward it, it alerts the downtrend is weakening.

2. Relative Strength Index (RSI)
The Relative Strength Index (RSI) is any other famous momentum indicator. Also an oscillator, the RSI acts as a metric for fee modifications and the velocity at which they alternate. The indicator fluctuates backward and forward between zero and one hundred. Signals may be spotted by means of buyers and analysts in the event that they search for divergences, failed swings of the

oscillator, and whilst the indicator crosses over the centerline.

Any rising RSI values above 50 sign wonderful, uptrend momentum, though, if the RSI hits 70 or above, it's regularly an indication of overbought situations. Conversely, RSI readings that decrease beneath 50 show bad, downtrend momentum. If RSI readings are beneath 30, even though, it's miles an illustration of feasible oversold situations.

three. Average Directional Index (ADX)

Finally, the Average Directional Index (ADX) should be mentioned. In reality, writer Welles Wilder installed the Directional Movement System – including the ADX, the Minus Directional Indicator (-DI), and the Plus Directional Indicator (+DI) – as a collection that would be used to help measure each the momentum and course of fee actions.

The ADX is derived from the smoothed averages of the -DI and +DI, which can be themselves derived from the comparison of two consecutive lows and their respective highs. The index is the portion of the

Directional Movement System that acts as a metric for the power of a trend, no matter its route. It's critical to notice that with the ADX, values of 20 or higher recommend the presence of a fashion. For any analyzing lower than 20, the marketplace is regarded as "directionless."

Chapter 6: Trend Following

Data is a treasured resource for groups and businesses. By studying statistics, you could advantage insights into consumer conduct, marketplace developments, and different elements that assist you to make knowledgeable choices. However, analyzing information can be a complicated and difficult manner. In this weblog publish, we will offer pointers and techniques for identifying traits and styles for your facts, so that you can make the most of this valuable aid.

Collecting Data

Before you may pick out trends and styles in your statistics, you want to gather it. There are many special strategies of information collection, such as surveys, interviews, and automatic statistics collection equipment. Regardless of the technique you choose, it's vital to collect relevant and accurate records. You should additionally organize and keep information nicely, so it is able to be without problems accessed and analyzed later.

Data Analysis

Once you've got accrued information, you need to research it to identify traits and styles. There are many different methods of records evaluation, which includes statistical analysis and system studying. The method you choose will rely on the type of information you have and your desires for analysis. For example, in case you want to identify correlations among specific variables, you can use statistical evaluation. If you need to expect destiny traits based totally on past statistics, you can use device gaining knowledge of.

Visualizing Data

Data visualization is every other vital tool for figuring out trends and styles in your information. By the usage of charts, graphs, and other visualization equipment, you may quick perceive trends and patterns that won't be at once obvious from raw information. There are many different varieties of visualization tools, and the one you select will rely upon the form of information you have and your desires for analysis.

Identifying Trends and Patterns

Once you have gathered and analyzed your data, you may start identifying trends and styles. A fashion is a widespread direction that a fixed of facts factors is shifting in, at the same time as a sample is a habitual theme or behavior within the information. There are many special forms of developments and styles that can be recognized in statistics, which includes seasonality, cyclicality, and anomalies.

To identify developments and patterns on your statistics, you can use information analysis and visualization gear. For example, you could use a line chart to visualize the fashion for your data over time, or a scatter plot to identify correlations among exclusive variables. It's important to interpret traits and styles within the context of your enterprise or corporation, so that you could make knowledgeable decisions based at the insights you benefit.

Taking Action

The insights you advantage from figuring out traits and patterns in your information may be used to make knowledgeable selections. For example, you can use facts to optimize your advertising campaigns, enhance your products and services, or lessen expenses. By taking action based totally on the insights you gain out of your facts, you can improve your commercial enterprise operations and reap your desires more efficaciously.

Using indicators and chart patterns to confirm trends

In the dynamic world of day trading, making informed decisions quickly and accurately is crucial. Indicators and chart patterns serve as essential tools for traders, helping to confirm trends and enhance trading strategies. This chapter delves into the various types of indicators and chart patterns, explaining how to use them effectively to confirm trends and make profitable trades.

Understanding Indicators

Indicators are mathematical calculations based on the price, volume, or open interest of a security. They are used to forecast financial market direction. Indicators fall into two main categories: leading and lagging.

Leading Indicators: These provide signals before a new trend or reversal occurs. Examples include the Relative Strength Index (RSI) and Stochastic Oscillator. Leading indicators are useful for predicting price movements and helping traders to enter trades early.

Lagging Indicators: These follow price movements and are often referred to as trend-following indicators. Moving averages and MACD (Moving Average Convergence Divergence) are common examples. Lagging indicators are beneficial in confirming trends after they have been established.

Key Indicators for Day Trading

Moving Averages (MA): Moving averages smooth out price data to identify the direction of the trend. The two most common types are Simple Moving Averages (SMA) and Exponential Moving Averages (EMA). Traders often look for crossovers between short-term and long-term moving averages to signal potential entries or exits.

Relative Strength Index (RSI): RSI measures the speed and change of price movements. It ranges from 0 to 100 and is typically used to identify overbought or oversold conditions. An RSI above 70 suggests that a security is overbought, while an RSI below 30 indicates it is oversold.

MACD (Moving Average Convergence Divergence): MACD is a trend-following momentum indicator that shows the relationship between two moving averages of a security's price. The MACD line crossing above the signal line indicates a bullish trend, while crossing below suggests a bearish trend.

Chart Patterns

Chart patterns are formations created by the movements of security prices on a chart. These patterns are used to predict future price movements based on past performance. There are two main types of chart patterns: continuation patterns and reversal patterns.

Continuation Patterns: These indicate that the current trend will continue after the pattern is completed. Common continuation patterns include triangles, flags, and pennants.

Reversal Patterns: These suggest that a trend is about to change direction. Head and shoulders, double tops, and double bottoms are typical reversal patterns.

Key Chart Patterns for Day Trading

Head and Shoulders: This is a reversal pattern that signals a change in trend direction. It consists of three peaks: a higher peak (head) between two lower peaks (shoulders). A head and shoulders top indicates a bearish reversal, while an inverse head and shoulders signals a bullish reversal.

Triangles: Triangles can be ascending, descending, or symmetrical and are continuation patterns. An ascending triangle, characterized by a horizontal top and rising bottom, usually precedes a bullish breakout. A descending triangle, with a horizontal bottom and descending top, often leads to a bearish breakout.

Flags and Pennants: These are short-term continuation patterns that occur after a sharp price movement. A flag looks like a small rectangle that slopes against the prevailing trend, while a pennant resembles a small symmetrical triangle. Both patterns are typically followed by a continuation of the previous trend.

Combining Indicators and Chart Patterns
Using indicators and chart patterns together can provide a more comprehensive analysis of market trends. For example, a trader might use moving averages to identify the overall trend and then look for chart patterns that confirm this trend. Similarly, combining RSI with chart patterns can help confirm overbought or oversold conditions before making a trade.

Example Strategy: A trader identifies an ascending triangle pattern, suggesting a potential bullish breakout. They then use RSI to confirm that the stock is not overbought. Finally, they wait for a moving average crossover to further validate the uptrend before entering the trade.

Practical Application and Case Study

Consider a scenario where a trader is analyzing a stock showing an inverse head and shoulders pattern, indicating a potential bullish reversal. By using the MACD indicator, the trader observes that the MACD line has crossed above the signal line, confirming the bullish trend. Additionally, the RSI is around 40, suggesting the stock is not overbought. The trader decides to enter a long position, anticipating a price increase based on the combined signals.

Managing risk in trend following

Risk management is a critical element of any buying and selling method, especially in trend following. While identifying and following tendencies can cause widespread income, it additionally entails inherent risks. This bankruptcy focuses on the standards and strategies for managing danger efficiently in trend-following techniques. By know-how and implementing those techniques, buyers can defend their capital and enhance their possibilities of lengthy-term fulfillment.

Understanding Trend Following

Trend following is a buying and selling approach that seeks to capitalize at the momentum of an present market trend. Traders who use this method accept as true with that securities which have been rising will maintain to upward push, and people which have been falling will continue to fall. The aim is to pick out and enter trades within the route of the trend and preserve the placement until the fashion suggests signs and symptoms of reversal.

The Importance of Risk Management

Without proper risk management, even the most successful fashion-following techniques can result in massive losses. Effective chance control allows buyers restrict their losses, defend their capital, and maintain emotional stability during buying and selling. It includes putting predefined regulations and sticking to them, irrespective of marketplace situations.

Key Risk Management Techniques

1. Position Sizing: Position sizing is the technique of figuring out how an awful lot of a security to shop for or sell. It is important to make certain that no single exchange can drastically effect the dealer's common portfolio. A common technique is the fixed-percentage model, in which a dealer dangers simplest a small percent of their general capital on any unmarried alternate. For example, risking 1-2% of the total buying and selling capital on each change guarantees that multiple losses in a row won't use up the dealer's account.

2. Stop-Loss Orders: Stop-loss orders are crucial gear for managing chance. A prevent-loss order routinely closes a function while the fee reaches a exact level, proscribing the trader's loss on that alternate. It is critical to set forestall-loss ranges based on the safety's volatility and the trader's risk tolerance. Placing stop-loss orders too near the entry charge can bring about premature exits, even as putting them too a way can result in large losses.

3. Diversification: Diversification involves spreading investments throughout unique securities, sectors, or

asset lessons to reduce danger. By diversifying, buyers can mitigate the impact of a bad-performing security on their universal portfolio. In trend following, diversification may be completed via trading a couple of securities that show off different trends, reducing the likelihood that each one positions will pass towards the trader concurrently.

four. Risk-Reward Ratio: The hazard-reward ratio measures the potential reward of a change relative to its risk. A common rule of thumb is to aim for a chance-praise ratio of as a minimum 1:2, that means that the capability income ought to be at the least two times the ability loss. This guarantees that although a trader wins simplest half in their trades, they can still be worthwhile in the end. Evaluating the chance-reward ratio before coming into a change helps traders make informed decisions about whether or not the potential praise justifies the risk.

5. Trailing Stops: Trailing stops are dynamic stop-loss orders that regulate with the fee motion of the security. As the fee actions inside the dealer's choose, the trailing forestall movements with it, locking in income while

nonetheless permitting the trader to capture additional gains if the trend maintains. Trailing stops are mainly beneficial in trend-following techniques, as they allow investors to live in worthwhile trades longer at the same time as protective in opposition to surprising reversals.

Psychological Aspects of Risk Management

Managing danger is not best about employing technical equipment however also about keeping the proper psychological mindset. Emotional discipline and adherence to threat control rules are vital for long-term achievement in fashion following.

1. Overcoming Fear and Greed: Fear and greed are commonplace emotions that may result in terrible decision-making in buying and selling. Fear can also reason buyers to go out trades upfront, while greed can lead to overtrading or maintaining positions too lengthy. By sticking to predefined hazard control rules, buyers can mitigate the impact of those feelings on their trading selections.

2. Consistency and Discipline: Consistency and area are vital in hazard management. Traders need to adhere to their hazard control strategies consistently, even if tempted to deviate because of marketplace situations or current buying and selling outcomes. Maintaining field helps investors avoid impulsive decisions that can lead to giant losses.

three. Learning from Mistakes: Every dealer makes mistakes, however a hit investors analyze from them. Keeping a trading journal to document trades, decisions, and outcomes can offer valuable insights into what works and what doesn't. Analyzing beyond trades facilitates traders refine their hazard management techniques and avoid repeating the identical mistakes.

Case Study: Risk Management in Action
Consider a trader who follows a fashion-following method and identifies an upward trend in a selected stock. The dealer comes to a decision to go into a protracted function and makes use of the constant-percent model to decide the placement size, risking 1.5% of their total capital. They set a forestall-loss order

three% below the entry fee, primarily based on the stock's volatility.

As the inventory charge rises, the trader uses a trailing prevent to lock in profits, adjusting the prevent-loss level because the price moves better. The dealer also diversifies with the aid of simultaneously trading other shares in exceptional sectors, lowering the hazard of a single stock adversely affecting their portfolio.

By adhering to their danger management plan, the trader is capable of defend their capital at some point of a marketplace pullback and capitalize on the general upward trend, in the long run attaining a profitable final results.

Chapter 7: The Psychology of Trading

Trading psychology refers to the mental kingdom and feelings of a dealer that determines the achievement or failure of a exchange. It represents the elements of a dealer's behavior and traits that have an effect on the movements they take whilst trading securities. While other elements – which includes experience and trading expertise – have an effect on the achievement of a dealer, buying and selling psychology is an essential issue that may make or destroy a change. Some of the feelings and feelings that traders revel in are useful, while different feelings including anxiousness, fear, and greed can hurt trading achievement and need to, therefore, be contained.

Traders who recognize trading psychology will typically keep away from making selections based totally on feelings or biases. It can assist them stand a higher hazard of incomes a profit for the duration of a trade, or inside the worst-case situation, reduce the quantity in their losses.

Basics of Trading Psychology

Trading psychology is distinctive for every dealer, and it is encouraged through the trader's emotions and biases. The primary emotions which are probably to impact the achievement or failure of a change are greed or worry.

Greed is described as the excessive preference for earnings that would have an effect on the rationality and judgment of a dealer. A greed-inspired change may also involve buying stocks of untested corporations because they are at the upward thrust or buying shares of a organization without knowledge the underlying investment.

Greed can also make a trader stay in a position for too long in an try and squeeze each event out of the trade. It is common on the end of a bull marketplace when buyers try and take on risky and speculative positions to benefit from the marketplace movements.

On the opposite hand, worry is the alternative of greed and the cause why people exit a exchange prematurely or refrain from taking up volatile positions due to concerns of incurring losses. Fear makes investors act irrationally as they rush to exit the exchange. It is common all through bear markets, and it's far characterized via giant selloffs from panic-selling.

Fear and greed play an crucial function in a dealer's universal strategy, and knowledge a way to manipulate the emotions is critical in turning into a a hit trader.

How Bias Affects Trading

Bias is defined as a predetermined disposition of 1 function over any other. Usually, whilst the dealer is biased, it may prevent right selection-making when buying and selling due to the fact it may save you a proper judgment. The trader may also end up appearing on feelings instead of on fundamental evaluation.

A trader is in all likelihood to exchange an asset or currency they've skilled achievement with in the beyond or keep away from an asset with a records of loss. Understanding such biases can assist investors conquer them and act with a calculated mindset.

The key forms of biases that affect trading consist of:

1. Negativity bias

Negativity bias makes a trader greater willing to the bad side of a alternate in preference to considering both the tremendous and poor aspects of a change. The impact of this kind of bias is that a trader may want to forego an entire method due to the terrible component after they handiest want to make a small adjustment to the method to show the change into a profit.

2. Gambler's fallacy

The gambler's fallacy is defined as an faulty perception that a selected event is much less in all likelihood or more likely to occur due to beyond events whilst it's been installed that the opportunity of such activities taking place does not depend upon the preceding activities. In such a case, a dealer can also assume that because a selected forex's been gaining, the fashion will keep.

three. Status quo bias

The popularity quo bias occurs whilst a dealer assumes that antique trades or strategies will hold being relevant within the cutting-edge marketplace. The risk of such an assumption is that the dealer does now not explore new opportunities that are relevant within the contemporary market, and it may doubtlessly lock them out of greater viable trades and techniques.

Improving Trading Psychology

Traders can enhance their buying and selling psychology via figuring out their very own emotions, biases, and tendencies that could determine a exchange's fulfillment or failure. Here are a few methods that buyers can use to enhance trading psychology:

1. Identify personality trends

A trader ought to perceive character developments early enough and plan how to overcome the terrible trends whilst actively trading so they do now not make decisions without a strong technical evaluation. Equally, buyers ought to pick out the positive trends that could help them make calculated movements for the duration of their time on the market.

2. Create a trading plan

A trading plan serves as a blueprint to your buying and selling, and it need to spotlight the desires that the dealer intends to acquire, the risk-praise ratio, and the buying and selling approach that they may be most cushy with.

For example, the trader can dedicate unique trading periods each day, set profit goals, and set a forestall loss to scrap feelings out of the technique. When growing a buying and selling plan, buyers should remember particular factors which include emotions and biases that may affect their capacity to stick to the plan.

3. Conduct research

Before investing in a stock, technology, or business enterprise, investors must devote enough time discovering and reviewing the possibilities. They should be on pinnacle of the news, have a look at charts, examine alternate journals, and perform industry evaluation.

Where viable, traders ought to attend webinars, trading seminars, and meetings to share and engage with other traders and finance experts.

Managing emotions

Common feelings in trading

While the emotional spectrum of a individual may be significant and deep, buyers generally distinguish 14 key trading emotions. These generally are available cycles, from excitement and euphoria, to fear and panic, and then despondency and melancholy.

Let's test the key emotional points of a trader's adventure.

Euphoria

Euphoria, or the sensation of extreme pleasure or elation, might be provoked by means of a profitable change, or a winning streak. While in the outside world euphoria typically has positive connotations, in buying and selling it could be a double-edged sword and lead to a distorted notion of capacity for widespread gains.

In the kingdom of euphoria buyers should grow to be greater self-confident and fall prey to the overconfidence bias, taking extra danger than they commonly would. For instance, investors may additionally take a larger function than they're cushty with, or use higher leverage, which magnifies each profits and losses.

Fear

In trading, fear might be precipitated through surprising market volatility. It ought to cause buyers to emerge as fixated on quick-term losses, prompting them to base choices on stressful mind rather than sound analysis. This may want to lead to a panic-pushed promote-off, with trader's ultimate positions or now not beginning positions in any respect.

Fear could also result in paralysis, while confronted with uncertainty, investors may additionally turn out to be reluctant to act. This will be particularly damaging in rapid-shifting markets, wherein pace of response is important.

Despondency

Despondency generally comes after the panic and capitulation tiers are over, and a dealer is left in the feeling of deep depression, with their self-belief at its lowest.

Despondency could be due to a giant loss or a sequence of losses. In fact, several research have shown the dangerous intellectual results of financial issues, with a few psychologists suggesting that a financial loss can cause grief.

Traders inside the nation of despondency are more likely to grow to be fixated on disasters and lose self-belief, come to be greater liable to the loss-aversion bias or give up buying and selling altogether.

How feelings have an effect on your buying and selling selections

Cognitive biases: Emotional trading should result in some of cognitive biases inclusive of overconfidence and excessive danger-taking, or on the opposite, loss aversion and giving up on buying and selling, just to name some.

Impulsive decision-making: Impulsive choice ought to cause steeply-priced errors, lack of subject and oversight, leaving buyers probably uncovered to greater losses.

Loss aversion: Loss aversion should purpose buyers turn out to be fixated on brief-time period losses and keep away from buying and selling

How to control feelings in trading?

Mindfulness and meditation. A developing variety of buyers at the moment are embracing those practices to cultivate an extended recognition of their thoughts and emotions and trading primarily based on rational decisions.

Journaling. Diligently documenting trade choices, techniques, and emotional states may help traders in comparing their overall performance, figuring out styles, and rectifying emotional biases.

Positive self-talk. Consciously replacing poor thought styles with constructive, affirming statements ought to help buyers in bolstering their self-belief, retaining composure and minimizing the impact of emotional biases in choice-making.

Taking breaks. Periodic respite from the relentless stream of marketplace facts may additionally permit traders to step lower back, recalibrate their cognizance and advantage angle on unfolding events, enhancing intellectual readability and emotional control in buying and selling.

Seeking assist. Engaging with friends may provide an possibility to change insights, discuss techniques, and proportion stories, which in turn can assist bolster emotional resilience.

Developing a trading mindset

Success in day buying and selling calls for extra than simply technical skills and marketplace understanding; it demands a sturdy trading attitude. Developing a buying and selling attitude involves cultivating emotional discipline, resilience, and a strategic approach to buying and selling. This bankruptcy explores the psychological elements of buying and selling, offering insights and strategies to assist buyers construct a strong mental framework for steady fulfillment.

The Importance of a Trading Mindset

A dealer's mind-set notably impacts their decision-making technique and common performance. Emotional reactions to market movements can cause impulsive selections, ensuing in losses. By developing a disciplined and resilient mind-set, traders can hold cognizance, control pressure, and make informed decisions based on their trading method instead of feelings.

Building Emotional Discipline

1. Understanding Emotional Triggers: Recognizing what triggers emotional responses is the first step in constructing emotional subject. Common triggers include fear of loss, greed for profits, and frustration from missed opportunities. By figuring out those triggers, buyers can develop strategies to manage their emotional reactions.

2. Setting Realistic Expectations: Setting practical expectancies is critical for maintaining emotional stability. Unrealistic expectations, together with aiming for excessive income in a quick period, can lead to

disappointment and irrational selections. Traders need to set manageable dreams based on their experience, market conditions, and chance tolerance.

three. Developing a Routine: Establishing a day by day trading recurring enables create consistency and decreases emotional strain. A properly-based recurring consists of pre-marketplace evaluation, putting in place trading plans, monitoring the marketplace, and put up-marketplace review. Consistent routines instill area and offer a sense of manage over the buying and selling system.

Cultivating Resilience

1. Embracing Losses: Losses are an inevitable a part of trading. Embracing losses as mastering opportunities rather than screw ups is prime to growing resilience. Analyzing dropping trades to apprehend what went incorrect can provide valuable insights and assist improve destiny overall performance.

2. Maintaining a Positive Attitude: A fine mind-set helps investors stay inspired and targeted, even at some stage in challenging durations. Practicing gratitude,

specializing in progress as opposed to perfection, and celebrating small victories can enhance morale and foster a resilient mind-set.

3. Stress Management Techniques: Effective pressure management is essential for maintaining mental nicely-being. Techniques along with mindfulness meditation, deep respiratory physical activities, and regular bodily activity can help lessen stress tiers and enhance average emotional resilience.

Strategic Approach to Trading

1. Developing a Trading Plan: A well-described trading plan serves as a roadmap for choice-making. It consists of standards for getting into and exiting trades, risk control strategies, and guidelines for position sizing. Adhering to a buying and selling plan facilitates decrease emotional affects and preserve a strategic technique to trading.

2. Continuous Learning: The economic markets are continuously evolving, and continuous gaining knowledge of is critical for staying ahead. Keeping up with market trends, studying new buying and selling

strategies, and mastering from experienced traders can enhance a dealer's understanding and adaptability.

three. Journaling and Self-Review: Maintaining a buying and selling magazine lets in buyers to report their trades, choices, and emotions. Regular self-review enables pick out patterns, strengths, and areas for development. By reflecting on past trades, traders can refine their techniques and improve their overall performance.

Case Study: Developing a Trading Mindset
Consider a dealer who struggles with emotional field, frequently making impulsive decisions based on fear and greed. To deal with this, the trader begins with the aid of identifying emotional triggers and setting sensible expectations. They increase a everyday recurring that consists of pre-marketplace analysis, putting in place buying and selling plans, and put up-marketplace evaluate.

To build resilience, the dealer embraces losses as getting to know opportunities, maintaining a wonderful mindset and working towards strain control techniques.

They create a detailed trading plan and decide to non-stop gaining knowledge of by using analyzing market traits and new techniques. Additionally, the trader maintains a journal to file trades and emotions, often reviewing it to perceive regions for improvement.

Over time, the dealer's disciplined method and resilient mindset cause extra steady and worthwhile buying and selling effects.

Conclusion

we've got traversed the multifaceted panorama of day trading, delving into foundational standards, sophisticated strategies, and the critical psychological and threat management components that underpin a hit trading endeavors. This comprehensive adventure, from the fundamentals to advanced strategies, equips you with the tools and understanding necessary to navigate the dynamic and frequently unpredictable international of day trading.

Recap of Key Concepts

We started with an introduction to day trading, exploring its definition, benefits, and inherent dangers. Understanding the marketplace shape and order float laid the foundation for appreciating how extraordinary market participants have interaction and influence fee movements. Setting up a robust trading station, including choosing the right dealer, platform, and configuring essential software program, provided a sensible start line.

Technical evaluation, with its awareness on chart styles, technical signs, and candlestick styles, offered a deep dive into the equipment used to interpret market information and make knowledgeable trading decisions. Trading techniques, which include fashion following, range trading, and breakout buying and selling, have been explored in detail, highlighting how to perceive opportunities and manage danger efficaciously.

Advanced techniques, together with scalping, information and event trading, and algorithmic trading, improved our toolkit, demonstrating how to leverage diverse methods for one-of-a-kind market situations. Risk management and buying and selling psychology emphasized the importance of information and mitigating dangers, managing feelings, and developing a resilient trading attitude. Crafting a customized trading plan encapsulated the realistic application of these ideas, ensuring a dependable and disciplined approach to trading.

Practical Insights and Case Studies

Real-lifestyles buying and selling examples and case studies supplied tangible insights into the successes and challenges faced via traders. Analyzing historical trading scenarios and gaining views from interviews with a hit buyers enriched our expertise of effective buying and selling strategies and the significance of non-stop studying and version.

Creating Your Winning Trading Plan

As you pass ahead, the advent of a personalized trading plan is paramount. This plan have to embody your desires, strategies, risk control techniques, and overall performance assessment metrics. Continuously refine and adapt your plan based to your experiences and evolving market conditions. Stay disciplined, affected person, and centered in your lengthy-time period objectives.

The Path of Continuous Learning

Day trading is a dynamic area that calls for steady mastering and model. Stay knowledgeable approximately market developments, financial signs, and international occasions that can affect your trading strategies. Engage with buying and selling communities, attend webinars, and invest in in addition training to decorate your abilities and know-how.

Final Thoughts

Day buying and selling is both an artwork and a technology. It needs a combination of technical knowledge, psychological resilience, and a disciplined approach. As you embark in your trading adventure, remember that success isn't always completed overnight. It calls for willpower, non-stop learning, and the capability to adapt to changing market conditions.

"Profit in a Day: The Essential Guide to Day Trading" has furnished you with a complete framework to understand, examine, and navigate the complexities of day trading. Armed with this expertise, you're well-ready to pursue your trading dreams with self-assurance and resolution. May your buying and selling adventure be marked with the aid of knowledgeable choices, strategic chance management, and persistent boom and fulfillment.

www.ingramcontent.com/pod-product-compliance
Lightning Source LLC
Chambersburg PA
CBHW071922210526
45479CB00002B/517